# Rosscarbery
## Past and Present

Edited by Patrick O'Donovan

Published by
Rosscarbery and District Historical Society
December 2001

Published by Rosscarbery and District Historical Society
December 2001

© Rosscarbery and District Historical Society

All rights reserved. No part of this book may be reprinted
or reproduced or utilized in any electronic, mechanical or other
means, now known or hereafter invented, including photocopying and
recording or otherwise, without either the prior written permission
of the Publishers or a licence permitting restricted copying in
Ireland issued by the Irish Copyright Licensing Agency Ltd,
The Irish Writers' Centre, 19 Parnell Square, Dublin 1.

ISBN 0-9541812-0-4

Printed by Skibbereen Printers Ltd
Design & Layout: Inspire Design

# Contents

| | |
|---|---|
| Sean Hayes 1886-1928 | 1 |
| The History of Lisavaird Co-op | 9 |
| St. Fachtna's College | 21 |
| Morning on the Warren | 27 |
| The Rosscarbery Steam Engine | 29 |
| Joseph E. Kenny, MP, and the Parnellite Split | 33 |
| Parish Registers | 41 |
| Rosscarbery – A Maritime Look | 45 |
| The Blind Boy | 49 |
| The Stations | 51 |
| The Rosscarbery Slate Industry 1830-1954 | 55 |
| The Capture of Rosscarbery RIC Barracks | 67 |
| Pairc A Tobair | 73 |
| Sand Dredging in Leap | 87 |
| Afternoon | 90 |
| The Importance of Children and Young People | 91 |
| The Drowning | 95 |
| The Sweeney | 99 |
| The Big Fair | 103 |
| Paul Daly - Stonemason | 105 |
| The History of Trotting | 109 |
| Rathbarry and Castlefreke | 115 |
| Glandore Classic Boat Regatta | 125 |
| First Autumn History School | 129 |
| Diary | 132 |

# Sean Hayes 1886-1928

*by Mary Coughlan and Sean Crowley*

Sean Hayes was born at Cregg, Glandore. His father was Denis Hayes and his mother was Catherine O'Donovan from the Lake, Kilkerran, who died in childbirth, or soon afterwards. Denis Hayes subsequently married another Catherine O'Donovan of Gortnadihy and they had four children, Maria, Bridget, Peter and Julia.

Sean attended school at Glandore under the tutelage of J. Barry. This school, along with Ardfield's Madden and Clonakilty's Crowley and Blewitt, were noted for the quality of their teaching. They prepared boys for the Civil Service in England. This was a popular career path in those days. Michael Collins and Sean Hayes went to London in the early 1900's to take up this employment. They socialised with fellow Irish emigrants and soon joined Irish organisations, Gaelic Athletic Association (GAA), Gaelic League and the Irish Ireland Movement.

The outbreak of War in 1914 meant the postponement of the Home Rule Bill. The Irish Parliamentary Party, under John Redmond, maintained their faith in a successful outcome. The National Movements, Irish Citizen Party, Sinn Fein and Irish Republican Brotherhood (IRB) had other ideas. They cited the failure of peaceful efforts, the Land League and Parnell, and decided that nothing short of an armed insurrection would succeed, especially now that England's attention was concentrated on the War in Europe.

Early in 1916 it became increasingly obvious that general conscription would include the Irish immigrants. Those involved in the national movements, who had not already left, returned to Ireland in early 1916. Their aim was to fight for Irish Independence.

Sean Hayes worked in the GPO and continued to participate in

*Sean Hayes*

activities of the Irish Volunteers and Sinn Fein. Michael Collins worked at Craig Gardener's, having already been employed at a London accountancy firm. Recruitment was actively continued throughout the country for the Volunteers and Sinn Fein. Meetings and drilling were openly held under the watchful eye of the authorities and the suspected leaders were arrested and deported repeatedly, causing public sympathy for those involved and increasing support for their cause.

The Irish Parliamentary Party continued to believe that Home Rule would be granted in spite of Carson's insistence that the nine counties of Ulster would be excluded.

The enormity of the loss of life on the Western Front, including tens of thousands of Irish men, prompted the British Government to recruit elsewhere, including Ireland. The Conscription Bill was passed and the still-trusting Irish Parliamentary Party gave its support. The National movements and the population vigorously opposed this in general.

This situation accelerated the determination of the National organisations to hold an armed insurrection, in the full realisation that a military victory was not possible.

The IRB, which included Padraig Pearse, Eamonn Ceannt, Michael Collins, Piarais Beaslai and Sean McDermott, amongst others, was central to the exact date and time of the Rising.

*General View of Frongoch, Prison Camp, Wales*

*Sean Hayes – 1886-1928*

*First Dail January 1919 at the Mansion House, Dublin*

This was a secret organisation, which kept this date closely guarded. When the time arrived messages were sent to the various groups assembled at different locations.

This order was countermanded by McNeill and was the information which would reach Sean Hayes and others on Easter Monday morning. Shortly afterwards, while walking in Phoenix Park with a friend, he heard that the Rising had commenced and went immediately to the GPO to play his part. He is said to have been one of the last to leave after the surrender.

The captured prisoners were marched to the Rotunda Hospital and confined within the grounds before being distributed to various prisons in England. Ironically they were jeered by some onlookers en route from the GPO to the Rotunda.

Sean Hayes and Michael Collins were in the group sent to Frongoch prison, which was originally a distillery. Huts were erected across the road and were used to accommodate German Prisoners of War who were moved elsewhere in order that the prison could hold the Irish men.

Daily routines within the prison camp were organised by the prisoners themselves; group leaders were selected, with one overall leader and a spokesperson. The prisoners managed internal discipline and working arrangements. Frongoch had Michael Collins and De Valera was to be the leader in Lincoln. The recognition of these leadership qualities in both led to them being chosen subsequently in the Provisional government. Many prisoners concealed their identity by refusing to answer roll calls or sign identity forms. Releases were made

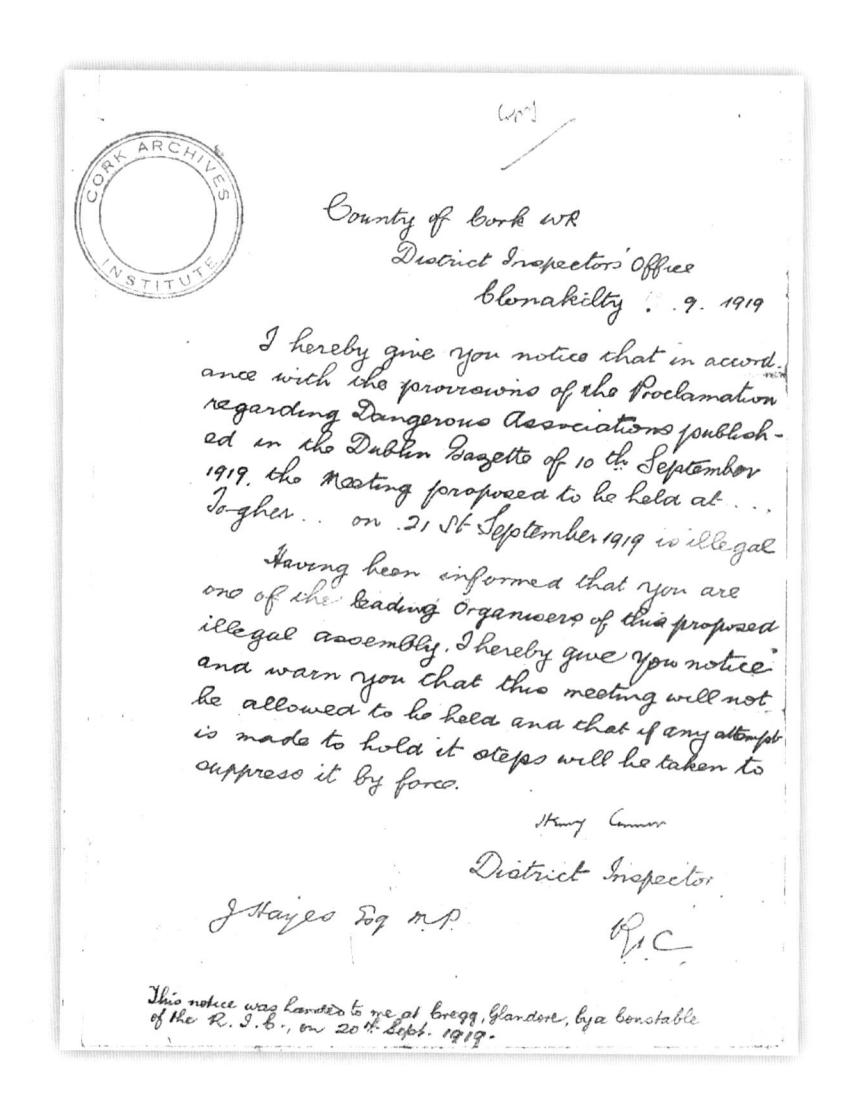

> County of Cork WR
> District Inspectors' Office
> Clonakilty 9. 1919
>
> I hereby give you notice that in accordance with the provisions of the Proclamation regarding Dangerous Associations published in the Dublin Gazette of 10th September 1919, the meeting proposed to be held at Togher on 21st September 1919 is illegal.
>
> Having been informed that you are one of the leading organisers of this proposed illegal assembly, I hereby give you notice and warn you that this meeting will not be allowed to be held and that if any attempt is made to hold it steps will be taken to suppress it by force.
>
> Henry Connor
> District Inspector
>
> J Hayes Esq M.P.
> R.I.C.
>
> This notice was handed to me at Cregg, Glandore, by a Constable of the R.I.C., on 20th Sept. 1919.

*The following letter showed that his movements were under constant scrutiny. I recall being told by Aunt Julia that he regularly concealed documents in the dry stone walls at the house in Cregg.*

gradually until December 1916 when the remaining six hundred were released under a general amnesty.

Sean Hayes returned to West Cork and continued to promote the National movement. He organised rallies and meetings with his colleagues all over the country.

He became editor and shareholder of the Southern Star in 1917, alternating with Ernest Blythe and Peader Hourihane. This newspaper was suppressed on several occasions, making its editorship a dangerous occupation.

The General Election in December 1918 resulted in Sean Hayes being elected TD for Cork West. The first meeting of the Provisional Government was held at the Mansion House in January 1919. The photograph of this group taken outside the Mansion House shows Sean seated second from the left on the front row. They expected to be arrested immediately for this defiant act as the police nearby were observing them. Some of those missing from the picture were still in jail.

The Southern Star minutes of 5 April 1919 show that Sean Hayes asked to be released from his editorship and he was succeeded by Peader Hourihane, Ernest Blythe having been jailed in March.

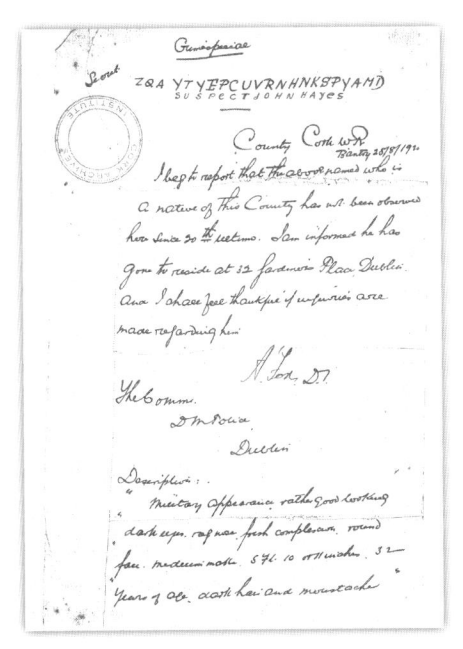

*Letter received by Sean Hayes at Cregg, 20 September 1919*

*Sean Hayes and his wife Ciss (Crowley)*

During the years 1919 and 1920 his activities were divided between Dublin's Provisional Government and West Cork, where he continued to hold meetings and rallies and was said to have been arrested several times.

A police roadblock was set up on the Drimoleague/Dunmanway road at Knockbue at a spot where the road crossed the railway line. The barricade was secured by using the railway gates closing the road. All passers-by were stopped and searched. From the Skibbereen side two cyclists appeared at some speed. On reaching the sharp bend on the road they found themselves confronted by the police. The cyclists were Sean Hayes and Michael O'Brien of Skibbereen, a prominent Sinn Fein activist. They were thoroughly, and somewhat roughly, searched under protest. However nothing was found on their clothing. They were about to be sent on their way when a policeman noticed the lamp on Mr O'Brien's bicycle. Inside they found a number of documents containing lists of volunteer names, designations and dates and venues of meetings, a valuable treasure trove of information for the police.

The Sinn Fein offices at 76 Harcourt Street were raided in November 1919 where the National Loan and other matters were being dealt with. Arrested were Jack McKee, Diarmuid Hegarty, Frank Lawless,

## Prisoners at Wormwood Scrubbs in 1920

*The photograph taken at the prison hospital shows a group that contains many West Cork names, Sean is seated between two nurses in the front row and was incorrectly listed as Sean Hayes of Tipperary.*

Sean Hayes and others. Michael Collins escaped through a well-prepared route through the roof and into a nearby hotel. Widespread arrests took place in 1920. Sean was one of those imprisoned in Wormwood Scrubs who was on hunger strike.

This Hunger Strike lasted eighteen days. The prisoners were all released under general amnesty later in 1920 and this led to the Treaty negotiations.

During the Dail debate for the acceptance Sean supported the motion in favour and seconded the proposal for its acceptance; the vote

*Picture taken at Newbridge Detention Camp shows Sean Hayes second from right and Michael Collins is second from left.*

*Sean Hayes (centre with moustache) pictured above attending the funeral of Arthur Griffith*

was carried in the Dail, also in a General Election that followed.

Civil war broke out soon afterwards, the pro treaty side led by Michael Collins and the anti group led by De Valera. Sean Hayes held the rank of Commandant in the army and was appointed by Michael Collins as Military Governor of Newbridge Detention Camp.

Sean married Ciss Crowley of Enniskeane in 1922. They resided at 28 Seafield Road, Clontarf. When peace was restored he took up an appointment in the GPO.

Failing health affected him in the following years. Sean and Ciss went to Switzerland in January 1926. At that time Switzerland was regarded as having an ideal climate for those suffering from respiratory illness. They returned to their home in Dublin in 1927.

Sean died in October 1928 of Pulmonary Tuberculosis following years of ill-health. He was 42 years of age. His funeral mass was celebrated by Fr. W. Mehigan and graveside prayers recited by his uncles Fr. P O'Donovan of Caheragh and Fr. D O'Donovan, Ballincollig. Michael Collins, a nephew of his great friend General Michael Collins, gave the oration at the cemetery. There is a plaque commemorating him on the gable of the present Glandore School.

*The headstone at Sean Hayes burial place, Glasnevin Cemetery*

# The History of Lisavaird Co-op

*by Pat Dineen*

Where did it all start? The first advocate of the Co-op Movement was William Thompson, who was born in Cork in 1775. His father, Alderman John Thompson, was a former Lord Mayor of Cork and High Sheriff of the County. When his father died in 1814 Thompson inherited a prosperous merchant business including a fleet of trading vessels and an estate of some 1500 acres in the townlands of Clounkeen, Three Gneeves, Carhogarriffe, Corran, Tullig and Cooladreen near Leap.

Thompson proposed to set up a Co-operative Community which would consist of some 2000 members. A Treasurer, Thomas Lyons, was appointed to take deposits and allocate shares, but before the venture could get off the ground Thompson died.

In his Will Thompson left £4000 to discharge any claims against his estate and gave an annuity of £100 to his lady friend, Anna Wheeler. The remainder of his estate was left to further the Co-op movement. His will was contested and the chief beneficiaries were the lawyers of that time.

The next great advocate of the Co-ops was Horace Plunkett and he was truly the founding father of the Co-op movement in Ireland. He was born in Dunsany, Co Meath, near the Hill of Tara, in 1854. He was educated at Eton and Oxford and, having completed his education, in 1879 he emigrated to Wyoming where he worked as a cowboy for ten years. He returned to Ireland in 1889 and set about doing something to improve rural Ireland. His slogan was Better Farming, Better Business, Better Living.

His first venture was to set up a Co-op Store in Doneraile in 1889. His comment at the time was that "The retail traders of Ireland, by their inefficiency, had lowered, rather than raised, the quality of rural life". Most stores had a bar attached and so the "curse of drink was added to the curse of debt". The venture failed however, mainly because of a Manager who could not communicate and a baker who could not stay sober.

Not daunted by this failure, the first Co-op Creamery was set up in Dromcollogher, Co. Limerick, in 1889. For the next 12 months, with the assistance of his first recruit, R.A. Anderson, he travelled the length and breadth of Ireland but met with no success and not a single further Co-op was established in 1890. However, better success came in the next year as 14 Co-ops were established. This did not happen without opposition and Plunkett's life was threatened on a number of occasions.

In 1892 Anderson addressed 440 meetings and by 1893 there were 30 Co-op Creameries in existence. It was now becoming evident that a co-ordinating body was needed to provide technical advice to Co-ops and also to advise on the marketing of butter. On 18 April 1894, during the Royal Dublin Society Spring Show, Plunkett and Anderson organised a Co-op meeting in The Concert Rooms, Great Brunswick Street, Dublin and immediately an organisation called the IAOS (Irish Agricultural Organisation Society), now ICOS (Irish Co-operative Organisation Society), was formed. By 1900 the IAOS had 840 affiliated Co-ops, of which 350 were Creameries.

The Co-op movement suffered greatly at the hands of the Black and Tans in 1920/21 as a convenient means of reprisal against Republicans. In 1920 the Tans started systematically burning Creameries,

*75th anniversay celebrations in 2000. Front l to r: Michael O'Callaghan, Charles Bateman, Denis O'Hea, John O'Donovan (Chairman), Pat Dineen (Manager), John Crowley, Margaret Mehigan. Centre l to r: Donal Tobin, Michael O'Donovan, Tim Hurley, Anthony Beechinor, Michael Collins, Sean Tobin, Richard White, Patrick Nyhan, Paddy O'Driscoll, Gerard O'Driscoll, Paud Donegan, Philip Cormac, Michael Dullea, Denis O'Donovan, Donal O'Sullivan, Leo Meade. Back row l to r: Denis O'Hea Jnr, Ted Coakley, Michael J. Santry, Michael Harte, John Kingston, Don Hurley, Dominic O'Mahony, David O'Brien, Frank Harte, Finbarr Collins*

*John Barry*  *Charlie Hodnett*  *Denis O'Hea*

leading to damage of an estimated quarter of a million pounds and loss of earnings of over one million pounds. From the outset the IAOS protested to government officials in Dublin and London. The British Co-op movement were also lobbied and helped to expose the atrocities which left many dairy farmers impoverished. Attacks on Co-ops abated as a result. In May 1921 a different tactic was employed and Creameries were closed by military order as a reprisal for disturbances. This came to an end in July 1921 with the declaration of a truce in Ireland.

In the early 1920's farming in West Cork was in a bad state. The price of butter fell drastically and the Cork Dockers Strike in 1923 closed the port and the export of cattle, live pigs and butter ceased. Not daunted, the farmers of West Cork chartered boats and exported live pigs from Bantry to Liverpool.

A group of West Cork farmers travelled to England and, having looked at the British market for Irish produce, they found that the market for home-made butter was hopeless but the market for Creamery Butter was very promising. They returned home and proceeded to consider the possibility of forming a Co-op Creamery. Many meetings were held and in 1923 Drinagh Co-op was established. The venture proved very successful and in 1924 a delegation from the Lisavaird area visited Drinagh and invited the Co-op to establish a branch at Lisavaird. This was considered and a local subscription of £1000 was sought to establish a branch. Further meetings were held in the kitchen of the Pike Bar and the project was turned down. Instead it was decided to proceed with the idea of forming a Co-op locally.

The first historical General Meeting was held on 13 March 1925. The meeting was well attended and the

*Jerry O'Donovan*  *John O'Donovan*  *John J. Calnan*

first Committee was elected. This Committee comprised: John Santry, Tullineaskey; David White, Tullineaskey; Jerry Collins, Tullineaskey; John Giles, Tullineaskey; Denis O'Sullivan, Clonlea; Hal Bennett, Ballyduvane; John Barry, Newmill; John O'Mahony, Coolnagay; Thomas French, Knockfeen; John O'Donovan, Balteenbrack, Ardfield; Michael F. Scully, Dunowen; Michael O'Brien, Curragh; Charles O'Neill, Ballyduvane. John J Calnan, Grancore was appointed as the first Chairman and Patrick O'Donovan, Balteenbrack, the local cow tester, was appointed Secretary.

An immediate decision was taken to build a Creamery. A plot of ground was purchased from John Giles, for which he got 10 £1 shares. An overdraft of £2000 was raised with the Bank of Ireland, Clonakilty, for which each Committee member had to become a Guarantor. The IAOS was contacted and they immediately sent down their organiser, Mr Courtney. They also sent their engineer, Fant, who advised on the buildings and machinery. Building was commenced and machinery installed at a cost of £1800. With the help of IAOS a Book of Rules was drafted for the guidance of the Committee.

The objectives of the Society were set out as follows:

a) To develop and improve the industry of agriculture by the introduction of improved methods, including the manufacture and sale of butter and other milk and farm products

b) To buy, sell and deal generally, wholesale and retail, in live and dead farming stock and produce, including fish, and in all kinds of agricultural products, seeds, manures, implements, machinery and general requisites.

c) To lease, purchase, hold, sell, rent,

*The History of Lisavaird Co-op*

Tom Hayes   Michael White   Finbarr O'Donovan

manage and develop, and otherwise deal with, land for farming or other purposes and to make all necessary provisions for the erection, repair, alteration or removal of all buildings, walls, fences and so forth, and to carry out any work in connection with road-making.

d) To hire or supply labour for the carrying out of agricultural or other work.

e) To provide for the housing of members and others

f) To make arrangements with persons engaged in any trade, business or profession, for concessions to members of the Society of any special rights, privileges and advantages, in particular to the supply of goods.

g) To advance or lend any of the capital or other monies of the Society, on satisfactory security, to members or others

h) To promote and encourage insurance by members in respect of accidents or injuries, malicious or accidental, to employees or to the property of members of the Society.

Membership rules stated that "The Society shall consist of members within a radius of 6 miles from Kilrovane Bridge, near Lisavaird. Applicants for membership shall pay an entrance fee of one shilling and subscribe for such number of shares in the Society as the Committee may in each case prescribe. No person carrying on any business similar to what the Society is engaged in shall be eligible to become, or continue, as a member of the Society." This is a very short extract from the Book of Rules which ran to over 40 pages, mainly dealing with meetings, voting, appointments etc.

The first employee of the Co-op was a man by the name of Thady Crowley from Carrigroe and the second man to be employed was Timmy

Sweeney of Tulligee. On 22nd August 1925 Maurice Curtin, from Tournafulla, Co Limerick, was appointed Manager. He previously held a position with Devon Road Co-op in Limerick. The number of employees grew to five during the first year of business. By the end of 1925 there were 80 shareholders.

Milk intake commenced on 5th August 1925 and the Secretary, Patrick O'Donovan, was put in charge of operations. In September 1925 the first Committee Meeting was held and it was decided to pay 7d (3p) per gallon of milk. In the first year of operation the Co-op handled 250,000 gallons of milk. There was immediate opposition from privately owned Creameries. The Hills, who owned a private Creamery in Clonakilty, opened a branch at The Pike in 1925. There were a number of other privately owned Creameries operating in Clonakilty, Rosscarbery, Knocks, Reenascreena, Ballinascarthy and Carhuvouler. Some were owned by the Hills and others by J.C. O'Sullivan, Clonakilty.

The first branch was built in Ardfield in 1927. This was followed in 1928 by a branch at Ballycummer (in the Lyre area). Carhuvouler branch was bought from J.C. O'Sullivan in 1929 and Clonakilty and Rosscarbery branches were acquired from Hills on 1st July 1929. Reenascreena branch was acquired in 1931. Union Hall was acquired from a private owner, John Sheehy, in 1936 and in the same year Glandore branch was acquired from a local Co-op group. Manch branch was built in 1939 and Ballinascarthy was acquired from the Cork and Kerry group in 1940. In many areas there were two creameries operating for a number of years until the Department of Agriculture intervened and forced the sale of the privately operated premises to the Co-ops.

In 1932 the Co-op entered into store trading and Charlie Hodnett from Rosscarbery was employed as Store Manager at Lisavaird. Store trading was gradually extended to all branches

John Barry, Newmill, succeeded John J Calnan as Chairman in 1932 and held that position until he died in 1959. In 1932 the Co-op changed its bankers from Bank of Ireland to the Munster and Leinster Bank because of a dispute about security for overdraft purposes.

In 1940 a forge was erected for the benefit of local farmers and in the same year an incubator, capable of hatching 2600 eggs, was installed. The incubator was worked with paraffin oil and was one of the first of its kind in the country. Day-old chicks were distributed all over Cork County. In 1942 a flax mill was erected. In 1952 the Co-op obtained a licence and commenced the manufacture of feed for pigs, cattle and poultry.

In 1953 Artificial Insemination (AI) was introduced and the first inseminator, Larry Collins, was employed. The Department of Agriculture kept Bulls at Darrara College. Maurice Curtin died in January 1955 and was succeeded by his assistant, Finbarr O'Donovan, a native of Ardfield.

In 1956 discussions were held with Bandon, Barryroe, Drinagh, Ballyclough, Ballinhassig, Killumney, Clondrohid and the Dairy Disposal Group in Aughadown and Terelton, and The South Western Cattle Breeding Society was formed, with its headquarters at Shinagh, Bandon. Michael White, who represented Lisavaird on the Board of the SWCBS, became Chairman at an early stage and held this position for almost 40 years until his retirement in 1996.

On 16 October 1957 Lisavaird was one of the first Co-ops to appoint an Agricultural Advisor, Jim Kiely. Michael White became Chairman in 1959 on the death of John Barry.

In 1965, in conjunction with Barryroe, Bandon, Drinagh, Dairy Disposal Aughadown and Carrigaline Co-op, a federation called Carbery Creameries was formed. The immediate task was to set up a cheese factory. A West Cork man, Bernie Cahill, Bere Island, was working with Express Dairies in London and, using this contact, discussions were held with Express and it was agreed to set up a cheese factory in West Cork. Ownership was 80% Express Dairies and 20% Carbery Creameries. A site for the factory was sought and the Lisavaird representatives, Michael White and Finbarr

O'Donovan, suggested a site at Burgatia. The site was considered suitable except for the caravans and mobile homes (which were very new at the time) parked at Ownahincha. The English delegations, afraid of such a tourist development in the locality, opted for a compromise site at Ballineen. The cheese factory was built and the first milk delivered to the factory in 1966 came from Lisavaird. The factory was a huge success, due in no small measure to an excellent milk supply and advanced technology, supplied by Express Dairies. Bernie Cahill was the first Manager at the factory. Gradually the factory was extended and skimmed milk power, whey powder, alcohol, other food ingredients and Mozzarella cheese were added to the products produced.

In 1971 the Co-op purchased a farm at Kippagh, near Reenascreena, and a pig unit was erected. By March 1973, 3200 pigs were in place for fattening. (A herd of 80 top-class heifers was pur-

*Committee Outing 1952: Front row l to r: James O'Hea, Jerome O'Brien, M O'Brien, Peter O'Donovan, James O'Driscoll, John O'Neill. Middle row l to r: John O'Donovan, Patrick Santry, Michael Harte, John Wilson, Jeremiah O'Donovan, Matthew Harte, John Crowley, John E Barry, Jeremiah Collins, Tim Joe O'Donovan, Daniel Mulcahy, John L O'Sullivan. Back row l to r: Michael J. Cooke, John Kingston, Maruice Curtin, James O'Mahony.*

*Maurice Curtin*    *Michael Cooke*    *Bernie Cahill*

chased in Northern Ireland and a Dairy Unit was also set up). The unit was extended later to carry 5000 pigs and this extension was officially opened by the Minister of Agriculture, Mark Clinton, on 25th September 1975. Later that night Mr Clinton was Guest of Honour at the Co-op's 50th Anniversary celebrations in Paddy Connolly's hotel in Ownahincha. Over 800 people attended the function, which went off without a hitch. The indoor swimming pool was covered over so that all 800 could dine at one sitting.

In 1986 Finbarr O'Donovan retired as General Manager and was replaced by his assistant, Jerry O'Donovan. In 1989 a further farm was purchased at Derryduff, near Lisavaird, and a pig unit to carry 200 sows was built. The progeny were carried to bacon weight at this unit. By 1994 the supply of weaners had dried up, due to the fact that sows were no longer kept by farmers, so the unit at Kippagh was remodelled and converted to a unit for 550 sows, with the progeny also being carried to bacon weight

In 1989 Lisavaird Co-op, along with Barryroe and Bandon Co-ops, purchased the liquid milk plant Strand Dairy, now Clona Dairy Products Ltd, in Clonakilty.

Inevitably the progress of time brought changes. With refrigerated bulk tanks on farms taking the place of churns being delivered to local branches, rationalisations had to take place. The first branch to be closed was Carhuvouler, in 1988. This was followed in 1990 by Clonakilty and Glandore. The other seven branches remain as important trading centres for the local population. 1990 saw 100% refrigeration of the Co-op's milk supply, but even yet a few suppliers choose to deliver their milk in mobile refrigerated tanks to meet the collection lorry at the local branch or collection point.

In 1992 a proposal was put to shareholders to merge the four Co-ops, Bandon, Barryroe, Drinagh and Lisavaird. However the shareholders at Barryroe turned down the proposal and the efforts to merge failed as a result. Michael White retired as Chairman in 1990 and was replaced by DenMATK 25Hea. In 1991 the four Co-ops bought out the Express Dairy interest in Carbery Milk Products and took over full control of the factory.

The Co-op had a vacant site in Clonakilty and in 1996 the Committee decided to build ten houses on this site. These were erected in 1997 and subsequently sold off.

At the AGM in 1996 the Rules were updated. Up to this time Committee members held office for four years and could present themselves for re-election on a continuous basis. Under the new rules a Committee member now has to stand down after serving two terms consecutively.

In 1998 Jerry O'Donovan retired as General Manager after a lifetime of dedicated service to the Co-op. He was replaced by Pat Dineen, who had been Assistant Manager since 1986.

Denis O'Hea retired as Chairman

*Con Hodnett*

*Pat Dineen*

## The History of Lisavaird Co-op

in June 2000 and was succeeded by John O'Donovan, Kilkern, who incidentally is a nephew of the first Secretary, the late Fr. Patrick O'Donovan. Lisavaird Co-op was very fortunate over the years in having an excellent Chairman at all times. John J Calnan, John Barry, Michael White and Denis O'Hea all gave years of dedicated service to the Co-op. John O'Donovan has carried on that high standard and his commitment to the affairs of the Co-op is outstanding.

Over the past number of years Lisavaird Co-op has come under pressure from its shareholders and customers to erect a modern supermarket in Clonakilty. With this in mind the Co-op purchased 5.6 acres of land adjacent to the town in March 1999. Plans were drawn up for a shopping centre containing a supermarket, hardware store, garden centre and petrol station. A planning application was submitted to Clonakilty Urban District Council in December 1999. Unfortunately the application was turned down on 17 July 2000. The decision has now been appealed to An Bord Pleanala and an outcome is expected in the near future.

In 2000 the three Co-ops, Bandon, Barryroe and Lisavaird, which own Clona Dairy Products in Clonakilty purchased Ballinahina Dairy, which is a liquid milk plant in Cork, from Kerry Co-op. This purchase gives Clona further access to outlets in Cork City.

In September 2000 John Joe and Theresa O'Sullivan, Gurranes, Rosscarbery, won the National Protein 350 Competition. On 19th October an Open Day was held on their farm and about 800 farmers from all over Ireland attended. In the same competition Robert and Shirley Shannon, Droumgarriffe, Ballinascarthy, were the winners of the Winter Milk Category.

On 29 November 2000 Lisavaird Co-op ceased its butter making operation after 75 years of production. All milk from the four West Cork Co-ops is now processed at Carbery Milk Products in Ballineen. Whilst it is sad to see this change, the ever increasing economic pressures made the assembly of all milk from the four Co-ops on one site inevitable. This ensures that the four Co-ops continue to head the Farmers Journal milk price league as they have been doing for many years.

In 2000 Lisavaird celebrated its 75th anniversary. At this stage I would like to acknowledge the foresight and huge commitment of the founder members. Finally I would like to thank the Committee of Management, Shareholders, Milk Suppliers, Customers and Staff for their loyalty and support over the years.

*The closure of Rosscarbery creamery. 31-03-89. Left to right, Ray O'Reilly, Con O'Sullivan, Patrick Harrington and Tom Kingston.*

*Jer Hayes, Con Hodnett and Con O'Sullivan*

# St. Fachtna's College

*by Very Rev. Christopher Peters, Dean of Ross*

A local landmark, clearly visible on old photographs of Rosscarbery, is St Fachtna's College, situated beside the Cathedral in what was known as The Cathedral Precincts. The building was burnt down in 1921 but the school seems to have disappeared without trace. When I started researching for this article, repeatedly I drew a blank. Further research is needed and this present offering is very sketchy.

Visitors to the Cathedral will see boards in the Narthex listing various clergy. The information contained on them is the result, in no small measure, of the tremendous work done by Dean Charles Webster on the history of the Cathedral and Diocese of Ross. What is surprising, however, is the lack of general information on the College to be found in his works

One of the boards in the Cathedral lists the principals of the Diocesan School and St. Fachtna's College. Diocesan Schools were established under Tudor legislation to provide Grammar Schools in every diocese. The Lord Lieutenant appointed diocesan schoolmasters, though presumably on the Bishop's recommendation. The situation changed for these schools with the passing of the Irish Church Act in 1869, which disestablished the Church of Ireland. At that stage the school changed its name to St Fachtna's College. (The alternative spelling, Faughnan, is also sometimes used). Similar schools then became what are known as Endowed Schools, dependant on financial support from educational societies. Hence Cole, in his Church and Parish Records of 1903, writes "The old Diocesan Parochial School, which existed under the Establishment, has given place to St Faughnan's College, a flourishing school, under the Revd. Alan Edward Penrose French". We will return to Revd. French later.

The first name on the list of Principals of the Diocesan School is Thomas Goodman, with the date 1695. In that year he was nominated to the Vicar Choralship of the Cathedral. Bishop Dive Downes (Bishop of the United Dioceses of Cork and Ross 1699-1710) wrote "In the parish of Rosse the Vicars Choral have all the tythes of 22 plowlands, worth almost £40 per an. The tythes of the town of Ross, viz.: - gardens, etc belong to the Vicars Choral of Ross and are worth about 20s. per an. They have also the book money of the whole parish, worth about £4 per an." In 1831 the Report of the Commission on Revenue and Patronage calculated the corporate revenue of the Vicar Choral (by that stage there being only one) as £409.12s.9d. Yearly payments from this revenue included £35 to the Curate of the Chapter, £40 to the Reader of the Cathedral, £8 to the Schoolmaster and £4.4s.0d. to the school.

An interesting entry in the Cathedral Chapter Book under 1725 states "the Chapter being out of debt, the wall of the churchyard next the Brigadier's garden be the first work gone about. It states that the Brigadier, or his heirs, have a lease of a piece of ground between the Cathedral and the Brigadier's house "which plot lies on the east side of the store house and north of the pulpit". The Brigadier referred to is Brigadier Freke and the house and ground are those of the School I have been unable to discover when the school was built on this site.

After Goodman there is then a gap in the list until 1825 when George Armstrong was appointed. He had been Reader in the Cathedral from 1796 to 1818 and was Chancellor of the Cathedral Chapter from 1798 to 1837, the year of

*St. Fachtna's College*

his death. This again emphasises the close relationship between the School and the Cathedral.

1825 is a significant year because of the publication of the first Report of the Commissioners of Irish Education Inquiry. However, the information it contains tends to confuse rather than clarify. There are a number of schools listed and the entry, which most probably refers to the Diocesan school, refers to a "large commodious house". That certainly fits, as does the salary of the schoolmaster, given as £360, which is well in excess of the teachers in other schools. However the name given for the master is Rev. James White, instead of George Armstrong. What is further confusing is that no Rev. James White appears in any lists of Diocesan clergy.

Armstrong died in 1837 but the next named Principal is George Beamish, appointed 1849. However, he appears in the Cathedral Preachers' Book as Reader from 1835. Beamish was succeeded by James Wynne O'Callaghan in 1854. There is a delightful monument to him in the Narthex with the following inscription:

In memoriam of Revd. James Wynne O'Callaghan M.A.

Late Principal of the Diocesan School Rosscarbery who died January 6th 1877. Aged 67 years

He held the above appointment for 22 years and resigned it owing to failing health. He was peculiarly qualified to be an instructor of youth, as well from his rare classical and educational attainments as from a natural kindness of heart, which endeared him to his numerous pupils. In all his dealings he was greatly respected as a man of the utmost probity. A true Christian Pastor and a trustworthy friend.

Following O'Callaghan's death, John Berry took up the reigns in 1878. By then the Church of Ireland had been disestablished and the name of the school changed to St. Fachtna's College. The Principal came to be referred to as 'The Master' and was also a minor Canon of the Cathedral. Berry occupied the position for only one year and in 1880 became Principal of Fermoy College, from whence he moved again the following year to be Head Master of Portarlington School, where he remained until 1885. From 1888 to 1892 he was back in Fermoy as Head Master of the College there and then moved to England for the rest of his ministry.

George Bruton succeeded Berry in 1880. Bruton, a graduate of Keble College, Oxford, was Master of the College and a Minor Canon of the Cathedral until 1892 when he was appointed Rector of Rathbarry and Ardfield. William Warnock Smith came as Master from Albermarle College, Beckenham in 1893. He later went on to become Chaplain of St John's Free Church in Cork. This was an Evangelical Trustee Church and suggests an interesting shift in Churchmanship from his predecessor who, we can assume, would have been a product of the high Anglican Oxford Movement.

This brings us to the last Master, Alan French, B.A. (T.C.D.), to whom we have already referred. He was appointed in 1902. In 1903 in the reference in Cole, already mentioned, the College is described as a "flourishing school". The Revd. French was assisted by a staff of three masters. However in an obituary written at the time of his death in 1943 it is stated that "he acted as headmaster of St Fachtna's College from 1902 until 1905". He was then appointed as Rector of Rosscarbery until 1914. At that time the present Deanery was the Master's house and, with the appointment of French as Rector, it became the Rectory. It was only in 1922, when the then Rector, Harry Becher, was also appointed Dean that the Dean became resident in Ross.

French's appointment as Rector in 1905 and his resignation as Master raises an interesting question since there is no record of a successor. Can we assume therefore that the College closed in 1905, or possibly kept going for a short while afterwards? But why should this school, which was said to be flourishing in 1903 close just two years later? I have no answer to that and Webster does not help us, even though he was writing only a few years later. In a guidebook he wrote in 1927 he lists significant dates in the Cathedral's history. While 1921 is recorded as the date the College

*Rear of College, showing racquet court.*

burnt down there is no reference to its closure. Also included is a photograph of the College dated 1914. Is it meant to imply that the College was still functioning, or simply that the photograph was taken in 1914? But why not then refer to it as the former College? At this stage I incline towards the 1905 date, although I would be very happy to be corrected. The fact that older residents have no recollection of the college functioning, or of seeing pupils around the place, tends to support his earlier date. The tantalising fact is that we are in the dark about an event of relatively recent history.

Another gap in the history is what the building was used for after it closed as a school.

What was life like at St. Fachtna's College? I am fortunate to have in my possession a Prospectus, which must have been written between 1902 and 1905, from which I take the following extracts:

THE SITUATION OF THE COLLEGE *is a most pleasant and healthy one, combining country and seaside, and specially suitable for boys, morally, physically and mentally.*

*Excellent safe sea bathing may be enjoyed during the Summer months, when the Head Master, or a responsible assistant, takes charge of the boys. The College is surrounded by extensive recreation grounds, including Tennis Court and Racquet Court, and care is taken to provide and maintain Cricket, Football and other games in their seasons.*

THE SCHOOL APARTMENTS *are lofty and well ventilated and include large Schoolroom, Class Rooms, Dining Hall and Spacious Dormitories.*

THE SANITARY ARRANGEMENTS *were arranged on the most modern and approved style at much cost a few years since.*

*A* VISIT TO THE COLLEGE, *and such visits are invited, will convince any parent that the health and comfort of the pupils are most carefully attended to, and for boys no better position could possibly be chosen for a Public School than that of the College.*

AGE FOR ENTRANCE *Those do best who are sent to St Faughnan's early, for careful grounding and continuous systematic training remove the necessity for any thing approaching over pressure, which for all boys it is essentially desirable to avoid.*

*The Intermediate examinations will not form the basis of education of the College, should parents specially desire their sons may be prepared for them*

THE SYSTEM OF WORK *adopted in the College is specially designed for such as require (1) a sound Preparatory Education, more especially for English schools; (2) A really practical Commercial Education; (3) a High-class Classical Mathematical or Scientific Examination. Pupils preparing for Universities, Professions, Civil Service and other Examinations will be worked specially for such, and every care will be taken that whatever is done will be thoroughly done.*

*Mr French may, under certain circumstances, and at special terms, take a few private pupils to read for Sandhurst, and for Militia preliminary Exams.*

The fees were £39 per annum for boarders under 12, £45 for boarders under 14 and £50 for boarders over 14. The names of some parents appear at the end of the prospectus and give an indication of the College's clientele: Colonel Galwey, R.E., Bellevue, Mallow; The Rev. Canon French, The Rectory, Strokestown; B.R. Purdon, Esq., R.M. Shepperton Park, Leap; Rev. S. MacConnell, The Rectory, Leap; J. Roy, Esq., Georgetown, Demerara, British Guiana, South America; W.F. Anderson Esq., Agent Bank of Ireland, Clonakilty; Ross Morgan Esq., M.D. Ballyfeard House, Kinsale, Co. Cork.

The college is long since gone and many questions remain unanswered about it. However on entering into the Nave of the Cathedral one is reminded of the College because of the inscription which reads:

*To the Glory of God.*
*The gift of friends and former pupils of St. Fachtna's College.*
*1927*

# Morning on the Warren

*By Eugene Daly*

This morning I strolled
on the Warren Strand.

The sun glittered on the water.
I could hear the ineffable
harp-strokes of the echoing sea.

I saw the sleek head of a seal
in the blue and gold morning.
Sanderlings shilly-shallied on the shore.

On a reef a cormorant stood
with wings outspread. The lapwings
called for rain, the plovers cried.

The hills were a blaze
of golden furze. A heron
stood priest-like at the water's edge.

As I turned to go, a flock
of sanderlings took flight,
bright flashes against the sky.

*Gone but not forgotten: clockwise from bottom left, Tom Galvin, Michael O'Mahony, Paddy Hayes, John O'Driscoll, Fachtna O'Donovan, Johnny O'Mahony, Kate Keohane and centre Vincent Daly.*

# The Rosscarbery Steam Engine

*by Michael John O'Mahony*

      *The Rosscarbery Engine*

You sons of old Rosscarbery, come listen for a while
Till I'll relate, this news of late, that came into our isle.
It's of the American Championship, held on Columbus' shore
Where our Irish boy, from them did fly, as he often did before

In October 1888, I'm sure it was the 6th
When on a Tuesday evening, the Championship was fixed
The race within was called for, these runners did prepare
And great was the excitement, that medal for to wear

When the men were ready, their backers loud did cry
The Yankee sang out to his man that day to win or die
The Corkmen they bet ten to one, that day within the ring
That O'Mahony from Rosscarbery, the Championship would win

As the men were on their marks, the trigger then they drew
And like some reindeers round the ring, those champion runners flew
For a hundred yards or more, the Yankee kept the lead
Until O'Mahony saw the tape, twas then he showed his speed

Though Moffatt struggled gamely, it was no use that day
He could not beat the Rosscarbery boy, well-known as by T.J.
He never yet was beaten, before in any ring
And wouldn't rest contented till the Championship he'd win

So now to conclude and finish, I must tell the people here
That O'Mahony in his form, could run with any deer
He is known all over Ireland, his praise is far and loud
And for a champion runner, Rosscarbery may feel proud.
                                              PD Mehigan

Timothy Jerome O'Mahony, also known as The Rosscarbery Steam Engine was born in the Carbery Arms Hotel (now the Ross Lodge & Tavern) in 1864. His father's name was Thade O'Mahony and his mother was Hanora McCarthy Cremeen from Milleen on the Lower Froe Road.

Timothy was educated at the Ardagh Boys School and as he grew to manhood he developed a perfect physique, which enabled him to compete with any athlete from any part of the world.

His athletic performances on the local tracks caused amazement, as his machine-like movements smashed all records and shattered the hopes of many would-be champions in any event he contested. It was for this reason he earned the name Rosscarbery Steam Engine.

### REBEL TENDENCIES

From his earliest youth he displayed strong rebel tendencies, which got him into trouble with the local Constabulary. After one particular skirmish in June 1888 he got fourteen days in Cork Gaol. On his release he was met at the prison gates by a group of dignitaries from Cork City and the officers of the Cork County Board of the Gaelic Athletic Association (GAA). He was given a Civic Reception by the Mayor of Cork, Ald. D. Horgan. The Skibbereen Eagle reported that he was attired in "Gaelic costume, consisting of a green jersey and knee breeches". When he eventually arrived back in Rosscarbery the members of the local football club, all wearing their playing costumes and carrying their hurleys on their shoulders, were out in force to greet him. An address of welcome was read by Geoff Wycherly, Secretary of the Ross National League. In this address O'Mahony was congratulated on his valour, sobriety and manly conduct as a true Nationalist and a worthy Irish man. James O'Callaghan, who chaired the gathering, also paid tribute to O'Mahony and his parents. A large force of police was drafted into town for the occasion, but their services were not required.

### ATHLETICS AND THE G.A.A.

When the G.A.A. was formed in November 1884 O'Mahony saw in it an opportunity to advance his own athletic career, as the G.A.A. took a very active role in the promotion of athletics in the early years. By this time O'Mahony was established as the leading quarter mile runner in West Cork. When the G.A.A. held their first All-Ireland Athletics Championships at Tramore, Co. Waterford, in 1885 O'Mahony won the 440 yds in 60 seconds.

In 1886 O'Mahony won the Irish Amateur Athletic Association (IAAA) 440 yds. in 53 2/5 seconds. The following year he was in the G.A.A. fold again, winning the 440 yds in 57 seconds in Tralee. In 1888 he bettered this time, winning in 53 3/5 seconds at a meeting held in

Limerick.

## THE GAELIC INVASION

The undoubted highlight of O'Mahony's career was his great success with the so-called Gaelic Invasion of America in October 1888. While in the States he won three races. The first was a quarter mile International Scratch Race at Beacon Park, Boston. The next was a half-mile handicap race at Madison Square Gardens, New York. The third race was for the American quarter mile Championship and this was also held at Madison Square Gardens. He won this race in 53 3/5 seconds. Although there was no World Championship then it is fair to say that O'Mahony's performances would entitle him to be ranked the number one quarter miler in the world at the time. Anyone who was able to win the American Championships would be regarded as World Champion. Needless to say he got a rousing reception on his eventual return home.

When he eventually retired from the track he devoted his time to promoting athletics and football under the auspices of the G.A.A. He was the first Secretary of the local Carbery Rangers club in 1887. He refereed matches and acted as handicapper and starter at sports meetings all over Munster.

By 1894 he had moved to Dublin where he continued his work for the G.A.A.. He also worked as a free-lance journalist and when the Dohenys of Dunmanway contested the All-Ireland Senior Football Final in 1897, the match report for the Skibbereen Eagle was written by T.J. O'Mahony.

After a number of years his health began to fail and he died on 10th September 1914 aged 50 years. The last word on the Steam Engine belongs to his friend and fellow journalist, P.D. Mehigan of Ardfield, better known as Carbery who paid him this generous tribute:

"A powerful and picturesque personality in the Irish Athletic world, and the greatest athlete which the Carberies has ever produced, with the possible exception of T.G. Wood of Enniskean, has passed to his reward during the week. T.J. O'Mahony, known all over these counties and in the States, as "The Rosscarbery Steam Engine" and referred to as Timothy in his native haunts, was buried in Glasnevin on Tuesday last.

To the younger generation of athletes The Steam Engine is only a name, but to athletes of a quarter century ago the pseudonym calls up a vision of exciting finishes and heroic deeds on every track from Dublin to Cape Clear, from New York to San Francisco. T.J. was perhaps the only one of that great team who reproduced his home form in America. His performance when beating the flower of the New World at Madison Square Gardens over a quarter of a mile will long live in the memory of his countrymen across the pond. It is hard to write calmly of T.J. O'Mahony. He himself was hypo-Celtic in temperament, excitable, honest, single-minded, warm-hearted – his virile personality dominated every gathering which he patronised. His early environment amongst an enthusiastic peasantry bred in him a vigorous (some would say extreme) National spirit, which knew no wavering. Little of the shrewdness, which is an essential factor in the makeup of a successful man of the world, was present in his character.

He lived and died a pure souled believer in Irish Nationhood. When his athletic prowess decayed he turned to his facile pen for support and whenever a Cork team travelled to Dublin we always looked for his clean-cut, well-clad figure at the Kingsbridge terminus. T.J.O. was always there. Standing some six foot plus and weighing fourteen stone, he suggested a combination of activity and strength unique in its blending. As a specimen of the man who went unsullied through all the mazes of a successful career he is a link which it is sad to close. His early demise is little less than a national loss. Of his victories we may have time and space to write in more peaceful times. For the present we can only say Beannacht De len a Anam"

*Denis and Betty Hayes with family and friends, pictured at his retirement party.*

# Joseph E. Kenny, MP, and the Parnellite Split in West Cork

*by Áine Ní Chonaill*

Charles Stewart Parnell towered over Irish political life as leader of the Irish Parliamentary Party, or Home Rule Party, during the last quarter of the 19th Century. His dramatic fall from grace, following the divorce case of William and Katharine O'Shea which revealed him as Katharine's long-time lover, is one of the most dramatic episodes in Irish history. Ireland split on a Parnellite and anti-Parnellite fault line in its aftermath.

What was the story here in West Cork, or more particularly in the constituency in which Rosscarbery was then located? A look at the political career of Dr Joseph E Kenny, who was elected MP for the constituency in 1885, will give us the answer as well as pointing up the enormous differences in electoral politics between then and now.

According to the constituency boundaries of the time, Rosscarbery was in the constituency of Cork South. This included the town of Clonakilty on its eastern boundary, Skibbereen on its western boundary and stretched north of Dunmanway, having the townlands of Coolmountain and Aultagh as its northern boundary.

Dr Joseph E Kenny was a Dubliner and had no connection whatever with the constituency of Cork South. In today's electoral politics in Ireland it is inconceivable that such a candidate would succeed in a rural constituency. Not only is there sharp competition between parties, but even sharper competition between candidates of the same party. This is due, in large part, to the competition engendered by our current multi-seat constituency system.

Things were very different in the Ireland of the 19th century. We were part of the United Kingdom which then, as now, had single-seat constituencies. This ruled out competition between candidates of the same party. Furthermore, Ireland voted Nationalist or Unionist. That was not a divide anyone ever crossed so, if the Home Rule Party put up a candidate in your area you voted for him if you were of Nationalist persuasion, irrespective of such details as what county he came from.

Another factor was that MPs were not paid by the State until 1911, so finding suitable candidates who

*Charles Stewart Parnell*

*Joseph E. Kenny*

were able to fund themselves was quite a challenge. The party was glad to find someone to slot into a constituency.

The Reform Act of 1884 expanded the franchise greatly and opened up the possibility of increased seats for the Home Rule Party. The hunt was on for suitable candidates and Parnell prevailed on Joseph Kenny to be one of them.

Kenny was close to Parnell. He was a medical doctor, born in Chapelizod in 1845. He had been on The Executive Council of the Land League and was in Kilmainham Jail with Parnell in 1881. He lived at No 15 Rutland Square East (now Parnell Square East) facing what is today the Garden of Remembrance. Then, as now, this was a political meeting place and Parnell frequently addressed a crowd from the window of Kenny's house. It was in that house, as Kenny's guest, that he was to spend his last night in Ireland in September 1891.

The Convention, to choose candidates for all the constituencies in County Cork for the forthcoming General Election in November, was held in Cork on 12 October 1885. Parnell and his entourage arrived at Cork Railway Station and were given a great welcome. They then retired to the Victoria Hotel where a preliminary conference was held. Parnell ran a tight party ship and Head Office expected to have its wishes followed. At the Convention Kenny, Edmund Leamy, John Hooper and WJ Lane were chosen unanimously. Difficulty was encountered with Dr CKD Tanner, JC Flynn and James Gilhooley. Eventually others withdrew their names and Head Office got its way. However, the next day the Freeman's Journal and The Irish Times referred to Parnell's dictation of candidates. The Cork Constitution declared:

"Mr Parnell is likely to hear a good deal about yesterday's selections and it may transpire that he will be constrained to make such alterations in the batch as shall, in some measure, mollify the indignation of a considerable section of his own supporters". However no such alterations were made.

Neither Kenny nor Leamy attended this Convention, a further indication of the cavalier attitude which candidates could take towards the electorate in those very different times.

Kenny was proposed to the Convention by Rev John O'Leary, Administrator of Skibbereen, and seconded by Cornelius Corkery. All candidates had to make a party pledge. Rule 6 of the Convention stated: If the person proposed is here, or within reach, he should there and then make a pledge. If he was not available his proposer would have to make the undertaking on his behalf. This was done on Kenny's behalf.

Because of the lateness of the hour Rev John O'Mahony, CC, Kinsale, proposed that the actual allocation of the candidates to the respective constituencies be left to Head office and so it was agreed. Thus delegates returned home, not necessarily knowing which of the candidates would stand in their particular constituency. The allocations were announced in the press on 14th October.

It will be noted that priests were very much to the fore in politics at that time. The Cork Examiner lists the names of all the clergy who attended in the order in which they arrived in the hall. There were about 150 clergy present. This was quite normal. The historian, Roy Foster, says that priests comprised on average one-third of the Convention's membership.

Branches sent four delegates each. The Rosscarbery delegates were TT Hayes, Tim Kearney, JJ O'Callaghan and J O'Donovan.

In the election Kenny was opposed by a conservative, F McC Connor. Kenny won handsomely with 4823 votes to F McC Connor's

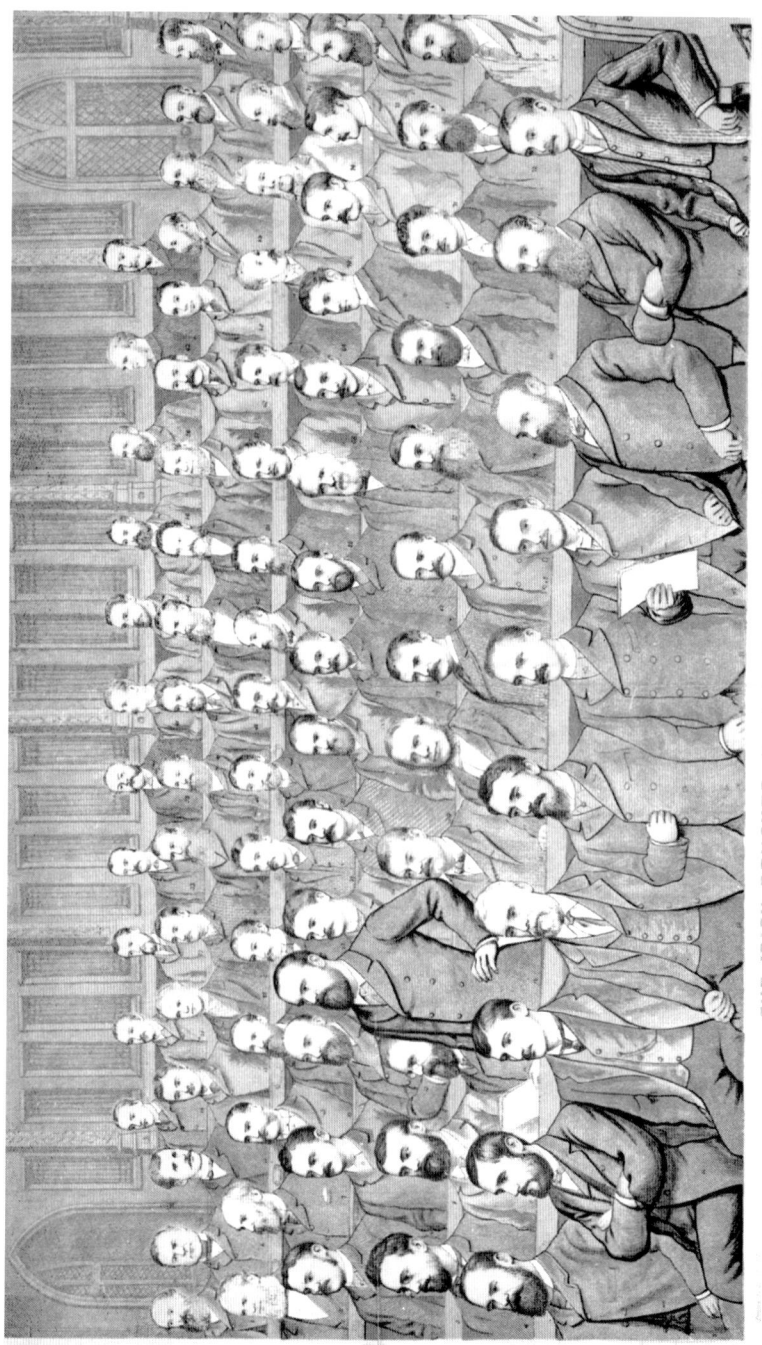

Rosscarbery - Past & Present

195.

A second election followed quickly in July 1886. This time sitting candidates in constituencies like Cork South were unopposed, so the election was merely a paper election with no actual contest. Nominations for the 1886 election were to be handed in to Skibbereen Courthouse between 1 o'clock and 3 o'clock on 9th July. The Cork Examiner of the following day reported: "Very little interest was shown in the proceedings, owing to there being no opposition. Though a rumour had got currency that Mr E Pike of Cork was to be nominated as a conservative candidate".

Three nomination papers were handed in for Dr. Kenny. The first was signed by His Lordship the Rt. Rev Dr Fitzgerald, Bishop of Ross, seconded by JJ Healy, solicitor. The second was signed by Rev John O'Leary, Administrator, Skibbereen, seconded by William Coakley, Ilen Valley Hotel, Bridge Street, Skibbereen. The third was signed by Michael Sheehy, CTC, Skibbereen, seconded by William Jennings, Bridge Street, Skibbereen. In each case there was attached a long list of "assenting voters". In the absence of Dr. Kenny, Fr. O'Leary proposed a vote of thanks to the Returning Officer.

I have come across no record of Dr. Kenny ever having visited the constituency over the next few years and am inclined to believe that he never did.

A monster meeting of the Irish National League was held in Rosscarbery on 29 January 1888 [1]. The posters advertising the event had promised that the two main speakers would be Dr Kenny and the famous Michael Davitt. In the event neither turned up. The crowd had to be content with speeches from

*Photo in Glasnevin Cemetery showing Kenny's grave beside Parnell's burial plot*
(Paul Kangley)

Rev. Hill of Rosscarbery, Mr O'Hea, MP, The Mayor of Cork, Alderman John O'Brien and Fr O'Leary of Skibbereen.

It was not such neglect of his constituents however that was to draw their wrath upon Kenny, but the stance he took in the Parnellite split.

After the debacle of the divorce case in November 1890 the party still re-elected Parnell as their leader in the leadership election which was customary at the beginning of Parliament. This, however, was before they learned that to keep Parnell as party leader would mean that they would lose the support of Gladstone for Home Rule. They could not achieve their aim without that support so they hurriedly held another meeting – the famous meeting in Committee Room 15 of the House of Commons. At this meeting the majority went against Parnell and, since Parnell would not accept his defeat, the party split. Kenny was the only MP from a County Cork constituency to vote for Parnell. He was extremely close to Parnell and never considered any other course of action. It was a personal position entirely at odds with the position of his constituents and they reacted with fury. An article in the Skibbereen Eagle of 20 December read:

*"Parnell – West Cork Unanimously Against Him*

*Priests of Bandon Deanery and the Crisis*

*We, the priests of Bandon Deanery, considering Mr Parnell's action in coming to Ireland to divide her people nothing short of treason on the field of battle, call on him and his followers to desist from that fatal course"*

The following motion from a party meeting in the constituency is typical:

*"We condemn the action of our representative, Dr. Kenny, in supporting a policy which does not represent the feelings of his constituents in South Cork, whose confidence he has therefore forfeited"*

A meeting of Dunmanway GAA said:

*"We call on Dr Kenny (our seldom seen representative) to*

support Mr O'Brien in his struggle to regain our national independence, or to resign immediately"

The Skibbereen Eagle gave accounts of similar meetings all over the constituency that week. There also appeared a letter to Dr Kenny from Fr. Coveney of Dunmanway:

*Dunmanway, December 15, 1890*
*Dear Doctor,*
*When would it suit your convenience to address your constituents in this district? They are anxious to hear you speak. De omnibus rebus et quibusdam aliis – i.e. Parnell's illness and the fire escape.*
*Yours truly*
*D. Coveney C.C.*[2]

Over the next few months meetings were held all over West Cork to dissolve local branches of the Irish National League (the official name of the party organisation up to this time) and replace them with branches of the Irish National Federation (the anti-Parnellite party).

Kenny did not resign of course. He continued to work doggedly in Parnell's cause.

Parnell's last visit to Ireland was in September 1891. On his arrival he sent a note to Dr Kenny from Morrison's Hotel saying he wasn't well. On 27 September he spoke at Creggs, Co Galway, in a terrible downpour. On his return to Dublin he spent three days in Dr Kenny's house attending to business. Kenny told him he was not well enough to travel but he insisted on going back to England, saying he would be back in ten days. He never saw Ireland again, dying in Brighton in the arms of Katharine, his wife since June, on 6th October 1891.

Another election was held in July 1892. Obviously there was no point in Kenny standing in Cork South. He stood instead, and was elected, in a Dublin constituency. He was one of only nine Parnellites elected. Parnell's support was almost exclusively limited to the Dublin area. In Cork South Edmund Barry, Newmill, Rosscarbery, of the Irish National Federation was returned unopposed.

Joseph Kenny died in April 1909. Although plots near Parnell's grave in Glasnevin were not normally available, friends of Kenny made a special request and the Cemeteries Committee allowed him to be buried quite near his 'Chief'.

## NOTES:

(1) Michael O'Mahony has reproduced an account of this from the Skibbereen Eagle in his History of Rosscarbery GAA. Pp11-12
(2) At the divorce case it was alleged that Parnell had sometimes used the fire escape to leave Katherine O'Shea's house if her husband arrived home unexpectedly.

## ACKNOWLEDGEMENT:

This article has its origins in research projects done for the Irish Times Young Historian Award by two former students of mine, Eleanor Jennings of Ballinglanna and Jacinta Collins of Knocks

## SOURCES

TM Healy - Letters and Leaders of My Day
Lyons FSL - Charles Stewart Parnell
Lyons FSL - John Dillon
Lyons FSL - The Fall of Parnell
Lyons FSL - The Irish Parliamentary Party 1890-1910
Eddie Marnane - History of Cork County Council
TW Moody - Davitt and Irish Revolution 1846-1882
Mrs Sophie O'Brien - My Irish Friends
William O'Brien - Recollections
FH O'Donnell - A History of the Irish Parliamentary Party
BM Walker - Parliamentary Election Results in Ireland 1801-1922
William John Fitzpatrick - History of the Dublin Catholic Cemeteries
Cork Examiner
Skibbereen Eagle

# Parish Registers

*by Fr. Pat Walsh PP*

Records in the church are almost as valuable as the building itself. The records contain the salient facts of the Christian life: Baptism, Confirmation, Marriage and death. Maintaining a record of one's life has been a pre-occupation of people far removed in time and culture from the Christian tradition. The old Gaelic ogham stones were often erected to mark a grave, and on these stones, in linear markings, were recorded the person's name and a fact or two about the person's life. In the early Christian tradition stones with ornamentation were preferred to ones with script. Later, for historical reasons, our burial places were marked with simple plain stones which may still be seen in so many old graveyards. There were people who could identify every stone with a particular family, but these "walking records" are fast disappearing. For the past 200 years or so gravestones with inscriptions have become normal.

Early Christian Ireland has left its legacy of annals, often more flowery than factual. These record the lives of the saints, scholars, kings and queens. They remain our main source of much of our early Christian history. As the Papacy grew more organised in medieval times so too appeared an increasing amount of documentation. Many of these papers are quite detailed with names of people, places and events. In the Roman archives are lists with every parish name and its townlands from this Diocese, a treasure trove for enterprising historians.

The purpose of this article is to present a broad introduction to the actual parish records we have here in Rosscarbery. They begin in two old-style copybooks. The paper is thick and has darkened with age. The script was written with a quill and later with a steel nib. The record of marriages begins in 1795 and that of baptisms in 1803. Similar records in most rural parishes date from this period, though in one parish in Cork there is a register going back to 1730.

The first recorded baptism here in Ross was that of James Buee (O'Donovan), a son of Patrick and Mary. His sponsors were Charles Sullivan and Mary Brien. The date was 10 January 1803. All the entries are in Latin. The townland of residence is not given. It would be interesting to see what the Latin version of Carraigfada or Ballyhoulihan would have been.

Another omission from these early entries was the maiden name of the mother. However in 1806 a new curate arrived. He obviously lived in a separate location from that of the Parish Priest because every quarter he arrived to register the baptisms he had performed during the previous three months. He included the mother's maiden name. So, for May 1806 we have the baptism of Hanora, daughter of Daniel McCarthy and Margaret Buee. This curate was Father George O'Hea. The appearance of the 'O' in his name is significant. At this time, and for many years afterwards, the 'O' is omitted from all surnames. The O'Hea clergy did not follow this practice for themselves but strangely they did not use the 'O' when recording their namesakes. Fifty years on when Father Michael O'Hea was Parish Priest here he begins to introduce the 'O' for his own family and for other families as well. We have O'Leary and O'Connor appearing in 1840 and O'Mahony in 1854. Father Jeremiah Moloney began the practice of including place names in the baptism register. Clever man, he did not attempt to Latinise any of these. So instead of writing "apud Rossensem" he just wrote "de Ross".

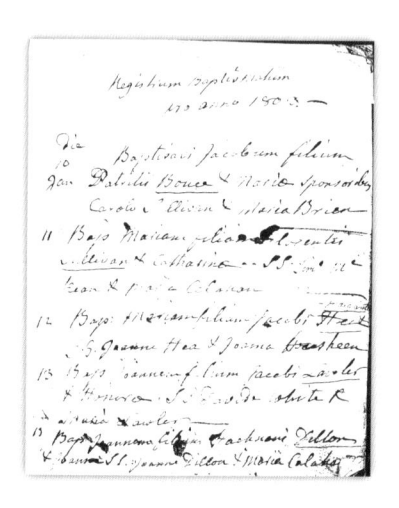

The first recorded marriage is dated 23 April 1795. Charles McCarthy, Kilmeen, married Catherine Riordan, Ross. The witnesses were Felix McCarthy, William Riordan, Daniel McCarthy and Father John Power. This record is especially interesting as it has the place of origin of both parties. Another interesting point about marriage records from this time is that the witnesses were men. This was a custom that endured almost to the end of the nineteenth century. My own paternal grandparents, for example, were married in Clonakilty in 1872 and the witnesses were the bride's father and the groom's uncle. Often there were numerous witnesses. The priest would write down four or five names and add that there were many others.

The two copybook-type registers, being small, are in good condition. The second baptism register – from 1820 to 1884 – is in folio format. The binding has long since melted away and the book is in poor shape. The second marriage register is in better condition but the writing is sprawled large across the unlined pages and is often almost indecipherable.

All the parish records, nationally, were microfilmed in the 1950's and the films are held in the National Library. It must be fiendishly difficult to decipher these prints. More recently an attempt was made to transcribe the registers, again on a national level. Post Leaving Certificate students were recruited and worked under trained supervisors. However, the young scribes were too often baffled by the texts and error-percentage was too high to allow the exercise to continue. Most parishes have done their own transcriptions and some have gone forward to having these on disc.

Here in Ross the marriages have been transcribed up to 1920 and the baptisms up to 1866. These transcriptions have recently been put on disc. It is a formidable task.

Firstly the writing. Handwriting is personal. Individuals and styles change. Ink fades. Often it amounts to conjecture but one hopes a happy and correct one is made. ur, un, or, ar, on and an are often indicated by a final flourish. y and g, m, n and r are often indistinguishable. When I first began to transcribe the older registers I was puzzled by the number of Ryan families residing in Mauliregan, for example. Had it been Tipperary this would have been understandable. Eventually I concluded that Ryan was in fact Regan. The eg had been merged to look like y. It is possible that the Parish Priest of Ballyporeen 200 years ago had the opposite writing quirk and made his y look like eg making Ryan look like Regan If so is it possible that President Reagan should have been visiting here instead? (On the question of American Presidents it is pretty certain that the late Rose Kennedy's ancestors (Fields) came from Courleigh North.)

Secondly, common use of sobriquets instead of the regular surname. There are names like Cahir and nothing more. Cahir is O Connor, Lohirt is O Driscoll, Mongane is O Brien. McCart is not a shortened version of McCarthy but, most probably, Dempsey. Bawn (Bán) could be anyone. We still have O Sullivan Bán, McCarthy Bán, O Driscoll Bán but then, as now, many families were fair-haired. There are other generic sobriquets as well. Reagh; McCarthy Reagh would probably put themselves higher in the pecking order over other McCarthys. So too would the O Donovan Reaghs. Reagh was used as a family name and who in fact were they? Most people fancy a tinge of blue blood. Dass, one of several to designate the O Briens. Likewise Blackstaff for the O Donovans. The O Sullivans, not to be outdone, with a resounding Blascagh. Not easy to sort them out 200 years on.

Thirdly, place names. To identify a place it is often necessary to identify a family. The registers of baptisms from 1812 onward have the townlands of the children included in the entry. Sometimes a name or a surname may have been omitted from a particular entry. By cross-reference to the place name it is possible to supply the omission. Quite a number of place names mentioned in the records are no longer in use. There are the obvious ones; Carraigagrianain (Sunnyrock), a lamentable change. Paulbeg-Pailbeg, which has been absorbed into Woodfield, again not a particularly glorious transition. Galtrage has been transformed into Millcove, so washing away centuries of history. Others have disappeared altogether. Lahirteedaniel —probably between Barleyhill and Cononagh; Milleen-Roe, between Tinneel and Ardagh; Cnocnamadoige, between Barleyhill and Reavileen. Some are not so readily identifiable. Where are Clashavuintuish, Glounvarcuish, Lisniname, Cnocanamrain, Parcnaseamroige?

Today the Baptism Register remains the single most important book in any parish. The historical event of ones Baptism is recorded just as ones biological birth is recorded in the civil registers. Some mistakenly believe that the Baptism Register is some form of parish roll book. Not so. Many baptised in one parish move away, even to other countries. Some, unfortunately, move away from the new life they have received. Later events in ones life are always sent back to ones parish of origin and so in the baptism entry the record of ones confirmation, ones marriage or ones religious profession is included. The other important register is that of marriages. As well there is a register of Confirmation and a register of deaths, though this last is not obligatory. It must be remembered that civil registers of births and deaths have been kept since 1876. However, for almost a century before that date the only reliable and comprehensive source we have is to be found in the parish register.

# Rosscarbery – A Maritime Look

*by Dermot Draper*

Looking out to sea from Rosscarbery one has a magnificent view of Galley Head Lighthouse and the Doolic Rock. To the east are the Crochna cliffs and Long Strand. Few would believe that over the centuries this area has become a graveyard of wrecked ships.

For instance, in the year 980, before the battle of Clontarf, a pirate galley sacked Ross Abbey and when leaving the harbour was wrecked on a nearby rocky headland from which it gets its name Galley Head.

From the diary of Elizabeth Freke dated 26th November 1693 she tells us that a great Dutch ship was cast ashore on Rathbarry Strand and was lost with every creature in it. Mr Freke found four bodies amongst the rocks and buried them in Rathbarry church.

On 1st April 1794 a Dutch galleon named Jeffrouw Neeltie drifted ashore and was wrecked on the rocks at Little Island Strand, Castlefreke.

The Maria of Plymouth, a brig, ran ashore on Little Island Strand on 15th March 1810. Within an hour she was dashed to pieces and all on board perished.

A most tragic shipwreck occurred on 8th January 1849 when the 900 ton barque Ceylon was wrecked on Crochna Rock. The Ceylon was bound for Boston and all its passengers were emigrants fleeing from the Famine and hardship. Only ten people were saved, seven males and three females. The reports of this wreck give us a detailed account of what our emigrants had to endure to get to the land of promise.

We usually associate gold and treasure with very old and historic wrecks but it is interesting to note silver dollars can be found on a wreck very close to home. The only vessel ever owned by the Liverpool & Mississippi Steam Ship Company was the Crescent City, a ship of 2105 tons built in Dumbarton in 1870. On 8th February 1871, on the return journey of her maiden voyage to New Orleans, she hit the Doolic Rock and sank. Her cargo consisted of 4100 bales of cotton, 3000 bags of maize and 40 boxes of Mexican silver dollars valued at £101,492. After the sinking, the cotton and some of the coins were salvaged. What was left, in today's

*Norwegian – wrecked off Red Strand - 1917*

value, could be worth about £120,000. It was as a direct result of this shipwreck that work began on building the lighthouse at Galley Head.

The Cecil, a brig, anchored in Ross bay on 8th February 1871 because of fog. Her anchor dragged and she was driven ashore. Coastguards from Dirkcove, Dunnycove and Millcove used their rocket apparatus to bring the crew to safety.

The Dewi Lass, a schooner, was lost at Long Strand on 7th May 1904. She carried coal from Newport to Clonakilty.

On 17th October 1928 the Plymouth ketch Flower of Portsay left the pier at Rosscarbery in ballast having discharged her cargo there. The ketch was bound for Appledore in Devon but was wrecked at Bullscove in Ardfield. The crew survived.

The nearest wreck to Rosscarbery occurred on Sunday morning 28th January 1865 when the Assaye, was wrecked on the Warren Strand in a severe storm. This ship is known locally as The Bombay as she was built in Bombay and sailed from there on a passage to Liverpool. She was a magnificent ship, built for the Royal Navy and made of teak. She was copper sheeted and copper fastened and her sides were pierced for 20 guns. The ship was sold out of the navy and bought by Messrs C. De Bourke and Co. as a merchant ship. The ship left Bombay on 11th

November 1864, sailed south across the Indian Ocean, around the Cape of Good Hope and into the Atlantic. She stopped at the island of St. Helena to collect the mails and replenish supplies of food and water. The ship sailed from St Helena on 15 December and a most favourable voyage was had until 20th January when she ran into severe storms. Fifty miles west of the Scilly Isles she sustained damage and the truss of her mainyard was carried away. Consequently the ship could not be steered properly and was blown in a northerly direction towards the Irish coast. At daybreak on Sunday 28th January land was sighted. It was the promontory of Glandore, but it was too late. Anchors were dropped, the sails were furled and desperate efforts were made to save the ship. The cables parted and the Assaye was driven on to the Warren Strand. The Captain volunteered to swim ashore with a line but he disappeared when halfway there and was never seen again. The rest of the crew, 48 in number, were rescued by a line set up by the coastguard. On Sunday evening the ship broke up and her cargo was scattered for miles along the shore. Some of it was salvaged by locals. The cargo at the time was worth £300,000. It consisted of 6254 bales of cotton, 556 bales of wool, 200 bales of jute and 93 tons of linseed.

*Ghazee – wrecked off Long Strand 1917*

The ship itself was worth £40,000. From time to time when old houses are being renovated in the town pieces of teak are often found as lintels, door frames and wallplates. These timbers are almost certain to be pieces salvaged from the Assaye, or as Ross people call it, The Bombay

### ACKNOWLEDGEMENTS:

Shipwrecks of the Irish Coast – Edward J. Burke

London Illustrated News

# The Blind Boy

*by Fachtna O'Callaghan*

Patrick Finn (Feen) was probably born in the vicinity of Benduff Slate Quarry as he was a nephew of two older Feen men, Patrick and James, and first cousin of the younger John, who were all killed in the disastrous quarry tragedy of 1892.

Patrick lived as a teenager with his widowed mother in a house by the main road at Derry. The ruin of this house can be seen today in the wood in front of Tom Herlihy's house. It was one of the Derry estate workmen's houses. His mother was a laundrymaid at Derry House.

After Patrick lost his sight as a young boy, the Townshends of Derry House had him sent to a convent school for the blind in Cabra, Dublin, to learn to be self-sufficient. There he was taught basket making and learned to play the fife and accordion.

Patrick and his mother later moved to West Rock above the town of Rosscarbery. Here he occupied himself making laundry baskets for the Cork laundries. He also grew potatoes and vegetables in a very steep garden up on West Rock behind Paddy O'Callaghan's house and shop. It was Paddy who gave me this information recently. He also told me that Patrick had helped him with his garden and that they drew dung into it with a gurry (a barrow with two sets of handles). On fine evenings Paddy and Patrick walked out the New Line and on Sundays they would walk to Mass.

Patrick Finn died in 1941 aged 64 years.

*Opposite page: Photo taken circa 1910. Front left:, Mrs Feen and son Patrick, Front right: unknown.*
*Centre: Two Scully girls; unknown pair; small boy, Dan O'Callaghan, Skibbereen Road; ?Hurley, Ardagh and Paddy Deasy, The Rock.*
*Back: Helena Cussen, Inchanoon (later Mrs Michael Cahalane, Droumihily) and Julia Hayes (later Mrs. Jerry Collins, North Square, Rosscarbery)*

Pioneers who received silver and golden pioneer pins in 1995 and 2000. Mary O'Mahony, Breda Goggin, Breda Hayes, Sr. Regina, Danny O'Sullivan, Fr. Martin Keohane, John Joe O'Sullivan, Sr. Ethna and John Hodnett, Pioneer Council.

Front from left, P.J. Tobin, Nellie May Collins, Denis O'Hea. Back, Fr. P. Walsh, P.P., Dermot Hurley, James Collins, Denis Hayes, Loretto Daly and Sr. Ethna.

# The Stations

*by Anne Cadogan*

I was reared in a village in West Cork in an era when there were very few television sets and those that existed received black and white pictures only. Colour televisions had not been invented yet, neither had microwave ovens, videotapes, computers or mobile phones. In fact, when I was about 12, our next door neighbours got an automatic washing machine. It was the first of its kind to enter the village, or surrounding townlands, so when word got out about the machine that would wash, rinse and squeeze the clothes by itself people trailed in and out of the neighbours' house for three days to see this extraordinary machine. In our small world Stations were an important part of our lives and culture.

For anyone reading this who would be unfamiliar with the word "Station" I will explain what it means. The Stations are held when the Parish Priest comes to a house in a townland to perform a religious ceremony of the Catholic faith called Mass. All the inhabitants of that townland come to the Mass and pay the Priest an offering called Station Dues. After the Mass, food, drink and entertainment are offered to all who attend. The owner of the house will often invite family, friends and relations to add to the crowd. In the past it was customary for the man of the house, and a few more important men, to dine with the Priest. The woman of the house had the very prestigious job of pouring out the tea. The Priest always got the first cup.

The lavishness of the Station would vary from house to house – depending on one's income and on how much one wanted to keep up with the Jones's, or even surpass them. It was not unusual for people to borrow money to cover the cost of the Stations. The motto was "Pray, eat, drink and enjoy the day" - and worry about the cost at a future time. Stations are still held in many places throughout the country but people are much more realistic about it and spend and do whatever they can cope with.

People like us, who lived in villages, never had to have The Station because of their proximity to the Church. They went there to pay their dues instead of the Church going to the house, as was the case in the country. For this reason it was a real treat for my family to be invited to a Station .

A lot of preparing had to be done for this big event, decorating inside and outside the house, broken window panes to be mended – some of them had been broken since shortly after the last Station was held at the house. Hedges had to be cut and the garden had to look good – sometimes a major rush job would be done here, a lot of shrubs and plants were placed in the freshly dug earth a few days before the big day. In addition there was the cooking and baking that had to be done – fast food and cooked meats had not yet become fashionable. The good china and cutlery (that was not used since the previous Station) had to be taken out of it's hibernation press, the dust washed off it to have it restored to its former glory. Sometimes items had to be borrowed from friends and neighbours, things like a big picture (the bigger the better; it did not have to match the rest of the interior décor) to cover up a damp patch on the wall that no damp proof remedies, or swears or curses, would remove. A fine big picture over this patch would make it seem non-existent to the guests.

People varied in their attitudes towards the Stations, some were well ahead of themselves and took months of systematic preparations for the whole event, whilst others had a slap-dash approach to the whole affair and all the work was done two or three days before the big day.

When I was in Secondary School it was the turn of one of my friend's family to have the Station.

My friend, her parents and granny fell into the slap-dash category. In fact granny lived by summer time all year round. She never changed the time on her watch and lived an hour ahead of everyone else in the household. In winter she had breakfast, lunch and dinner on her own. Isolation was the price she paid for being ahead of everyone else. The slap-dash approach meant being up until 2am painting and wallpapering and out again early in the morning gardening. As a result of lack of sleep, mounting tension and stress, and spending lots of money in a short space of time, tempers were well frayed and a lot of arguing, swearing and falling-out went on. My friend's parents had a major fall-out over the type of wallpaper to purchase.

Due to the mounting pressure I was drafted in to help on the day before the big event. No school for us that day. It was an early start polishing, dusting, washing floors upstairs and down. Carpets were not common then and one particular bedroom had to look really impressive because on the day it was to be the "coat room" where people would put their coats as soon as they arrived at the house. This also gave them a chance for a sneaky look

*The Stations*

around upstairs. In this room my friend and I stuffed everything that could be moved into a huge press. She leaned against the two doors whilst I tried to close them, hoping and praying that they would not cave in under the pressure from inside.

In the afternoon the cooking and baking had to be done and a man from Clonakilty came with a roll of new lino for the kitchen floor. Granny and I were assigned the job of making the trifle. Granny boiled some water and told me "go east to the calf house for the gallon bucket". I, being from the village, did not know where east was and did not want to show my backwardness by asking so I decided to go and search until such time as I found the calf house, which I eventually did. I brought back the bucket, which had leftovers of yellow meal in it from the last feed , and handed it to Granny. I assumed she would do a thorough job in cleaning it. Alas hygiene was not a priority with her and, to my astonishment, she put the bucket on the table, threw some sponge cake into it, tore open four packets of Birds strawberry jelly and flung them in on top of the cake. She then threw in some boiling water, no measuring jug here, or wooden spoon for that matter, and proceeded to stir the whole thing with a fuschia stick that she had broken from the hedge outside and trimmed down. This stick's only sterilisation was when it hit the jelly in the boiling water. After about twenty stirs the jelly was sorted and the stick was flung out the back door, landing on the hedge from where it came. Not wanting to be around to see how the custard was made I made an excuse and left the kitchen.

The following day we had a lovely Mass and everything looked well. I did not eat much and when asked if I wanted trifle I had to pretend I had already eaten too much and had no room for it. People remarked how lovely the trifle tasted and I thought to myself that the yellow meal residue must have added to the flavour.

Everything went off fine, except someone put their cigarette out on the lovely new floor covering, burning a hole and creating a scorch mark to last until the next Station. Granny said they should have waited until after the Station to put the new lino down.

There were no reports of anyone taking ill next day. Was it Divine Intervention?

*Junior C West Cork football final, left, Mike Keohane, Alan Ronan, Johnny Murphy, Rob Aherne, Eddie Hayes, Noel Hayes, James O'Sullivan, Ivan Jennings, Philip Moore, David Creedon, Anthony Roche, Micheal O'Sullivan, Brian McCarthy, Daniel Harte, Aidan Hayes, Con Hodnett, Sean O'Riordan, trainer Sean Keane, Newtown.*

# The Rosscarbery Slate Industry 1830-1954

*by Michael Tobin*

There were three phases in the development of the slate industry.

**1. 1830-1895: the dominance of the industry by Wales:**

From the 1850's there was a building boom in Ireland and Britain. House building in Dublin and Belfast was proceeding at a rapid pace. Most of the market in Ireland for roofing slate was supplied from North Wales, because the Irish quarries were remote from the main centres of demand and slate travelled more safely by sea than over land.

The Welsh slates had possession of the market for so long that a prejudice existed among builders and the public against the use of any other slate. In 1880, when the Parish Church in Rosscarbery was renovated, Welsh, rather than Benduff slates were used.

**2. 1895-1930: the dominance of American Slate:**

In the middle 1890's the quality of Welsh slate became suspect. Regular supplies were no longer assured, as the North Wales quarries became the scenes of prolonged and bitter industrial conflict. Builders began to look for alternative sources, and the United States quickly became a large source of supply. The U.S. had the advantages of low shipping costs, efficient selling techniques and an alert consular service i.e. their embassies did their utmost to promote the sale of American slate in these islands.

**3. 1930-1940: the dominance of Irish Slate in the home market:**

Protectionism became the universal policy during the inter-war period. World trade fell by more than 50%. Import duties decreased imports and encouraged domestic production. The output of Irish Slate quarries remained low until the 1930's. Then protected by a massive tariff of £5 a ton, imports declined and domestic output increased. However the boom lasted for only a few years, and by 1939 the West Cork slate industry was in a depressed condition, as Ireland was experiencing a depression due to the fall in international trade.

### The Rosscarbery Slate Quarries i.e. Benduff – Froe - Madranna - Cooladreen

*Development of the quarries*

It appears that a vein of slate was discovered at Benduff in 1812 when the new road from Skibbereen to Cork was being constructed. The road was to follow a straight course through the valley at Benduff, but it was constructed around the slate and consequently, it followed a very circuitous route.

The slate was situated in the estate of the local landlord, Morris, who lived nearby in Castlesalem. He brought experts from Wales to establish the quarrying industry in Benduff. The quarry was opened in 1830.

According to Jukes' Geological Survey in October 1860: "the quarry is worked for a depth of 70 feet near the road, and there are heaps of rubbish all around it.

The list of slates that are made and their prices:
Queens 26"to 36" high by different width:£6.10.0 per 1,000
1st Duchesses 24"by 12" £5.10.0 per 1,000
2nd Duchesses 22"by 11" £3.15.0 ditto.
1st Countesses 20"by 10" £2.15.0 ditto
1st Ladies 16" by 8" £1. 5.0 ditto
2nd Ladies 14" by 7" £1. 0.0 ditto"

In 1883 Benduff and Froe were the

*Photo taken at Madranna slate quarries probably in early 1930's, including Connie Donovan, Bill Cook, Jer Donovan, Michael O'Sullivan, James O'Sullivan, Charlie Cunningham, John O'Brien, Paddy Tobin, Tim Cullinane, Jimmy O'Regan, John Joe Hayes, Paddy O'Sullivan.*

most extensive slate quarries in Co. Cork. The number of men employed varied from 100 to 150. These quarries produced 2,600 tons of slate, which had an estimated value of £5,500. At that time the entire country produced 10,000 tons with an estimated value of £20,000.

According to Francis Guy's illustrated Descriptive and Gossiping Guide to the South of Ireland 1883:

"The Benduff and Froe Slate Company's Quarries are situated about one mile from Rosscarbery, and three miles from Glandore Harbour, where there are vessels of sufficient size to take the slate to any market. About one hundred, men and boys, are employed by the company this year, but more than double this number have been employed. Four steam engines have been placed on the works. The slates are of a dark colour, and very durable. Roofs in good preservation are to be seen which were covered fifty years ago (1830's) with these slates."

## OWNERSHIP OF THE QUARRIES

1830-65:
Morris of Castlesalem

1865-1891:
The quarries were owned by a company whose principal shareholders were; James H. Swanton, William Shaw, James Swanton, James C. Alliman, Jeremiah Mc Daniel, Henry Hitchmough, Henry Belcher, Samuel Jagoe and William Tower Towsend. The company also controlled the quarries at Froe and Madranna.

1891-1911:
By 1890 Benduff Quarry was in financial difficulties. In March 1891 the Munster and Leinster Bank, presumably to recoup losses, put in a liquidator in the person of Mr. Edward McCarthy, Accountant, who had offices at 16 Marlboro Street, Cork, and John French was appointed manager. The quarry was in liquidation from 1891-1911.

## THE DISASTER AT BENDUFF

On July 20th 1892 eight men lost their lives when one side of the quarry collapsed on them. The bodies of three men were removed, but the other five were never recovered. In addition two others were injured. According to the booklet, Disaster at Benduff, which was published in 1978 by the relatives of those who were lost, there were approximately fifty men and boys employed in the quarry at the time of the disaster. Most of the men had long experience in quarrying and were in a position to appreciate the normal dangers associated with the work. Their hours were from dawn till dark for six days per week for a wage of roughly eight shillings. There was no doubt whatever that they appreciated the danger they were in while working under the ledge which was eventually to take the lives of eight of them, so it is certain that these good men put the needs of their families beyond their own personal safety.

As early as February of 1892 a cleavage had been detected on the huge ledge under which a section of ten men normally worked. This had been reported to the owners and their response was to send a Bank Manager with no engineering qualifications whatever to inspect it. The Bank Manager stated that the crack posed no danger!

Whether it was premonition or some new evidence of imminent danger, on the evening before the disaster the men were very frightened about the condition of the huge ledge under which they were working. They expressed their fears to the Manager on that occasion, and, on the following morning, expressed them in even stronger terms. They were, however, given the option of work or the gate, and, once again, the fear of hunger overcame the fear of danger.

At 6.00 a.m. ten men; John Donovan (aged 16), Daniel Connor (50), Michael Tobin (49), Patrick Feen (60), James Feen (54), John Feen (25), Denis Dwyer (19), John Neill (13), James Mahony, and Jeremiah Connor moved under the perilous ledge and began their day's toil. They had been working about an hour and a half when, without any warning, the ledge collapsed burying the unfortunate men under more than 1,000 tons

*Fred Donovan, Barleyhill, foreman at Benduff Quarry.*
*(photo courtesy of Julia Mary Hayes, West Square)*

of rubble. Of the ten, only James Mahony and Jeremiah Connor survived, though with severe injuries. Subsequently the bodies of three of the victims were recovered by their gallant work-mates in the teeth of great danger to the searchers and in the face of a further collapse which nearly claimed them as well. These were the bodies of John Donovan, Denis Dwyer and John Neill.

After the disaster the quarry continued to operate under various owners up to 1950, and continued to give a fair measure of employment, sometimes numbering up to 100 men. However, during this period it witnessed further disasters, it claimed three further lives: John O'Regan, Benduff(1929), James Tobin, Barleyhill(1934) and Denis Dempsey(1937) all of the same stock as those who lost their lives in 1892.

The following article appeared in the Cork County Eagle & Munster Advertiser on 14th July 1900. The article was written by a journalist and gives us a look at the quarries from the employer's point of view. It appears that the journalist spoke only to the employer

*Benduff: Great West Cork Quarry (by our special commissioner).*

"At the Horse Show last week one of the first exhibits which met the gaze of the visitor after passing the turnstiles was that from the Benduff Slate Quarries. There was shown at the stall roofing slates in all sizes and of the very finest quality. Many of the large numbers of people, who stopped at the stall, expressed their surprise, that they were not aware of the fact that such beautiful slates, the equals in appearance in all respects, of the slates imported from Wales and from America, are procurable here in our own county of Cork. But knowledge of our local resources is not a strong point, with many of our people.

The quarries are situated some two miles to the west of Rosscarbery and ten miles from the town of Clonakilty. They are on the main road leading westwards to Leap, Glandore and Skibbereen. Worked for a long series of years, the business was interrupted some eight years ago, when a most lamentable accident occurred. The north wall of the quarry without any warning gave way, and five men were buried under the debris, their bodies never being recovered. For a time all work was suspended and there were those who thought that the renewal of operations would be so costly as to be absolutely prohibitive. To remove the great bank of debris, it was obvious from the outset, would cost an immense sum of money. But the present proprietor of the quarry, Mr. James Swanton M.A., Glandore, saw a way out of the difficulty, and recognised that if the quarry was to be profitably worked again new ground should be opened, and new methods adopted. The old machinery, which was of an elaborate and, for the times, of an efficient character, was evidently no longer available. He decided to leave the old machinery where it was, and adopted entirely new methods. To the eastward of the old working, over which the cliff had fallen, a vein of slate was discovered of the very best quality. The new method of working adopted by Mr. Swanton was what may best be described as the American Cable System. He was the first to introduce this system into these islands.

When I visited the quarry the other day I was able to observe the quarrymen carving out the slabs of slate rock, and to see these slabs being split by skilled workmen, and "dressed" by others. The quarrying, the splitting and the dressing are all going on side by side in the depths of the quarry. There is a great advan-

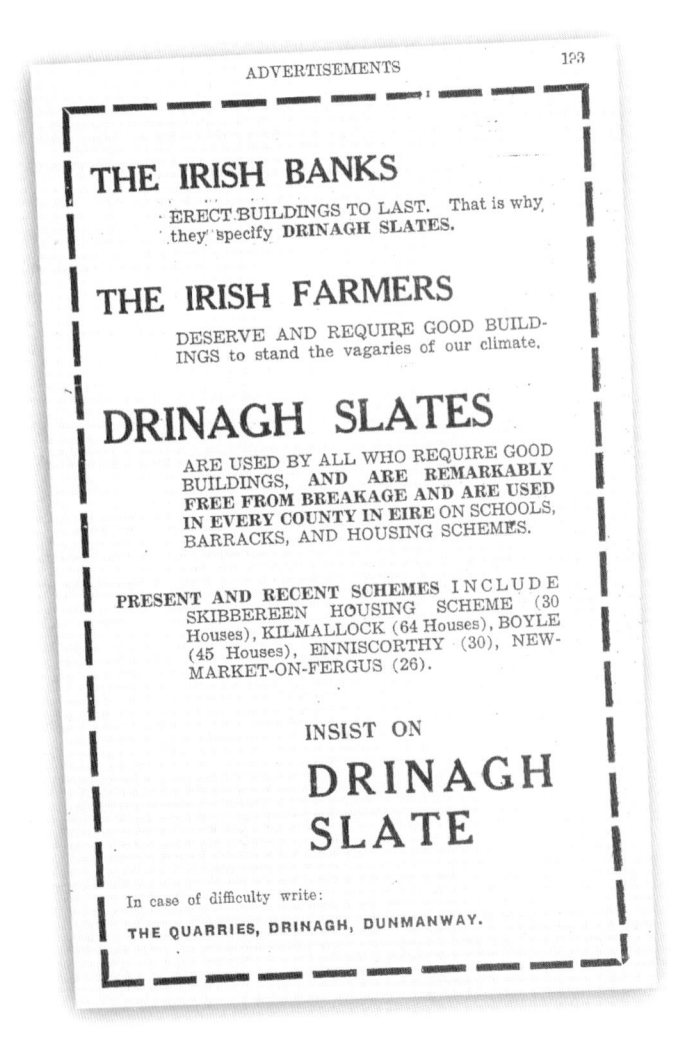

## THE IRISH BANKS

ERECT BUILDINGS TO LAST. That is why they specify DRINAGH SLATES.

## THE IRISH FARMERS

DESERVE AND REQUIRE GOOD BUILDINGS to stand the vagaries of our climate.

## DRINAGH SLATES

ARE USED BY ALL WHO REQUIRE GOOD BUILDINGS, AND ARE REMARKABLY FREE FROM BREAKAGE AND ARE USED IN EVERY COUNTY IN EIRE ON SCHOOLS, BARRACKS, AND HOUSING SCHEMES.

PRESENT AND RECENT SCHEMES INCLUDE SKIBBEREEN HOUSING SCHEME (30 Houses), KILMALLOCK (64 Houses), BOYLE (45 Houses), ENNISCORTHY (30), NEWMARKET-ON-FERGUS (26).

INSIST ON

## DRINAGH SLATE

In case of difficulty write:
THE QUARRIES, DRINAGH, DUNMANWAY.

*Advertisement for Drinagh slates.*

tage in this system of working. The rock splits better when it is fresh from the quarry, and there is therefore, very much less waste than there would be if the slabs had been left lie in the open air for any length of time. The workers are all local and there can be no doubt as to their skill.

There is one great drawback, which one meets too often in this country. The want of railway accommodation makes development difficult in the extreme. It is only necessary to look at a railway map of Cork County to see how Benduff is handicapped. The Clonakilty station is ten miles away and is placed "out of bounds" because of the hill by which it is approached. Skibbereen is about the same distance from the quarry but as the approach to the station is better it is by way of Skibbereen that the slate is sent to Cork. To the credit of the Cork, Bandon and South Coast Railway be it said that the company offers every facility for the transit of the slate. It actually costs more per ton to convey the slate by road to Skibbereen than it does to convey it by rail from Skibbereen to Cork.

For slate sent by sea the arrangements are, on the whole good. There is a special slate pier at Leap three miles distant, which at high tide can be approached by fair sized vessels. But, without a railway, there can be no adequate development of an industry, which is obviously capable of great expansion. What is wanted is a line of light railway from Clonakilty to Glandore, on the broad gauge system, to allow the trucks laden with slate, flags or fish to run through to Cork. As a matter of fact some years ago the Grand Jury of Cork County passed a guarantee in favour of a line from Clonakilty to Rosscarbery. But the government of the day did not rise to the occasion. Taking all the circumstances into account, this is eminently a case for state intervention and assistance. There is more wealth in the slate rocks of Benduff than there is in a thousand square miles of Uganda, on the railway for which millions of English and Irish money are being spent.

It is a crying shame that such a concern, as Benduff should be left without the assistance which private enterprise encourages and justifies. Let a railway line from Clonakilty to Glandore via Rosscarbery and Benduff, be made with the assistance of state aid and all will be well. Without that railway a veritable mine of wealth must remain undeveloped."

Railway Company's plan to extend railway line from Clonakilty to Benduff:

In his book Clonakilty a History the author Michael J. Collins states that the first train to Clonakilty arrived on 28th August 1886. The Clonakilty station was located high up on the edge of the town, because it was the intention of the management to extend the line westward as far as the slate quarries at Benduff and a hill-top location in town would make for the ideal take-off point for such a venture,. Such a railway, they pointed out, would enable those slates from the west to undersell in Cork the same commodity imported from Wales. The shareholder, who did most to push the Benduff project, was Horace Townsend, Derry, Rosscarbery.

The Benduff Quarry from the Workers' point of view, based on an interview with Johnny Tobin, Benduff in 1969.

The working day began at 7am. There was a break of three-quarters of an hour at 9am for breakfast. Work carried on until 2pm when there was another break of three-quarters of an hour for lunch. The working day ended at 6pm. They worked six days every week. At the beginning of the last century all workers got a half-day off in the week but they had to work some extra time during the week in order to earn this half-day.

The workers were paid according to the amount of slate they produced. The slate was transported out of the quarry in wagons driven by two steam engines to a storehouse near the road. There were five workmen in charge of each wagon, and each worker was paid two pence for every wagon of slate delivered.

Coal was used to produce the steam and in order to carry away the smoke from the quarry two very high chimney stacks were built, but only one of them exists today. The other chimney stack, which was near the road, was demolished in order to make room for road improvements.

In 1911 the average weekly wages were:

| | |
|---|---|
| The manager | 24/- |
| The assistant manager | 15/- |
| Foreman | 11/- |
| Quarrymen, slate cutters, slate dressers etc., | 10/- |
| Labourers | 8/- |
| Less experienced labourers | 6/- |
| Youths | 5/- |

Deductions were made from their wages if the workers were unable to work for some reason e.g. bad weather. It is interesting to note that the majority of the workers never got paid in notes during their life-time, even up to the 1920's, but in comparison with the workers of the present day (1969) their wages were sufficient to meet their needs as their standard of living was low.

The youths working in the quarry received very little education. They were allowed to attend the church for a few hours on certain days to learn prayers for their Confirmation, which they received when they were in their late teens.

1911-1919:

A Cork City company took over the quarry. They continued with the quarrying on a very big scale and installed modern machinery.

1919-1952:

A company consisting of Messrs T. Healy, Solicitor, P.J.O'Sullivan and Justin McCarthy took over the quarry. The quarry finally closed down in 1952. There were thirty-six workers

## The Rosscarbery Slate Industry 1830-1954

there at that time.

### The Cooladreen Slate Quarries from Guys' Postal Directory 1883

"The Cooladreen Slate Company's Quarries are situated near Leap. The quarries have been worked for the last five years by an English Company, which lately installed some expensive machinery. They employ about thirty hands at present but expect shortly to carry on operations on a much more extended scale. The slate is of good quality, and there is a large demand springing up in the country".

The slates produced in Cooladreen were small. The quarry closed in 1947 and the big crane was sold to the Killaloe Quarry.

### The Madranna Slate Quarries from Cork County Eagle 2nd October 1899

"The Madranna Slate Quarries are two miles east of Leap. The slates now being produced are perfectly free from iron stains and are admitted to be the best produced in Ireland, and are successfully competing with Welsh at prices from 30% to 50% lower". (The quality of Welsh slate had deteriorated by this time and the new competitors were the Americans).

The slates have been successfully tested by Mr. Cutler, Engineer to the city of Cork Corporation. Upon being tested for absorption of water, at the usual angle, they proved to absorb none.

Upon testing for strength they stand as follows:
First: Madranna slate bearing a strain of 90 pounds.
Second: Bangor bearing a strain of 83 pounds.
Third: Portmadoc bearing a strain of 54 pounds.
The test for splintering is, they do not do so, whereas Bangor and Portmadoc do.
Applications for price lists to be made to:
74, South Mall, Cork.
or to:
Captain Ellis, at Madranna Slate Quarries, near Leap, Co. Cork

The Ellis' were miners from Pendeen, Cornwall. They lived in Madranna House. In 1904 the last Ellis lady died in that house. Her daughter married Justin McCarthy, who lived in Sea View, Barley Hill. Justin was Manager of Benduff, Froe and Madranna Slate Quarries. His eldest son, W.G. McCarthy was foreman in Benduff until October 1915 when he took up a position with Vickens, Barrow-in-Furness.

Madranna had a longer life than Benduff. It was owned and managed by P.J. O'Sullivan from 1920 until 1954.

In 1932 the three quarries of Benduff, Froe and Madranna gave employment to approximately ninety workers.

### DRINAGH SLATE QUARRY

According to the book, "Neath the Blackthorn" by Johnny Keohane and

*Photographs taken from Drinagh Slate Quarry. (Courtesy of P.J. McCarthy, Reavouler, Drinagh)*

Karen Billing, Drinagh Quarry was in full operational service as long ago as 1867 but it closed for many years until it was taken over by the Hodnett family from Courtmacsherry and Rosscarbery in 1934. Jerry Hegarty (late of Fullers, Skibbereen) and Tommy Healy, State Solicitor, were also involved. Grants were acquired which enabled the quarry owners to improve machinery, production and manpower. The primary purpose of these grants was to relieve unemployment.

In Drinagh the slate was quarried off the cliff-face, but in the other quarries they worked downwards. Drinagh Quarry closed in 1962.

### QUARRY PROCESSES:

At the quarries the processes of extracting, splitting and dressing the slate took place. A very important part of the extracting process was the removal of rubbish or waste rock. It was not uncommon for up to 90% of rock to be disposed of in this way. Most quarries dumped the waste rock using end-tipping rubbish wagons over the nearest slope and the slate waste heaps thus developed, and these are the single most noticeable landscape-feature visible today.

The demand for quarry slate declined from the late 1930's. The slate was coarse and the builders had difficulty in roofing houses with it. It was also costly to transport. Today manufactured slate, which can be purchased in "builders' providers" has replaced it. This slate is thinner and lighter than quarried slate and it lies better on the roof.

### SOURCES:

Report of the Cork Industrial Exhibition 1883

Journals of the Economic and Social History of Ireland, 1974/75 & 1977.

Francis Guy's illustrated Descriptive and Gossiping Guide to the South of Ireland 1883

Juke's Memoirs (October 1860) to Sheet 200.

Interview with Johnny Tobin, Barley Hill in 1969.

Disaster at Benduff, compiled and written by David Walsh July 1978.

Cork County Eagle and Munster Advertiser:
I. July 14th 1900. Benduff Great West Cork Quarry
II. October 2nd 1899 Madranna Slate Quarries
III. January 27th 1917 Benduff & Madranna Quarries.

'Neath the Blackthorn by Johnny Keohane & Karen Billing

Notes on slate quarries in West Cork during the 1930's by Mr. McCloskey (Department Inspector) – Library of the Geological Survey of Ireland, Beggars' Bush Barracks, Dublin, 4

Clonakilty A History by Michael J. Collins.

*Denis O'Leary with specimen pollock caught off Millcove*

# The Capture of Rosscarbery RIC Barracks

*by Con O'Callaghan*

The British had boasted that Rosscarbery Royal Irish Constabulary (RIC) Barracks was one of the safest fortifications in the country and one that the IRA could not capture. In saying this, they more or less issued a challenge to the IRA. If it could be destroyed, the Flying Column would have a large area from Clonakilty to Skibbereen without a major enemy Barracks.

The Flying Column was a group of IRA volunteers selected from throughout the Brigade area, which is roughly from Bandon to Castletownbere. Included in this Flying Column would be a hard core of regular fighters, but the personnel changed from time to time as each Company area had men prepared to take their place in the Column. The Column was divided into sections with a leader in each.

The first attempt at Rosscarbery Barracks never materialised. On Feb 1st 1921 the Flying Column marched towards Rosscarbery. The Column Commander, Tom Barry, decided to billet his men in Burgatia House (now the home of the Maguire Family) about a mile from the Barracks, so that they would be fresh for the attack on the Barracks. There were a number of reasons for staying in this house:

(1) the convenience of the House to the Barracks.

(2) The owner of the House, Thomas Kingston, was (in the words of Tom Barry) "a British Loyalist", and he thought it was time to feed the Column at his expense rather than at cost to loyal supporters of the IRA.

(3) If the Column had been seen moving towards Rosscarbery, the British would never think of looking for them in an a loyalist house.

The Column arrived at Burgatia House at 3 am. The postman, Jerome Scully, arrived early the following morning. They knew this man was not on their side. He was brought in for questioning and swore to tell nobody of the presence of the IRA. He was released at 12.30pm but on his return to Rosscarbery, he informed the RIC. By 4pm the Column sentries reported Black and Tans moving along the road in front of the House and a few minutes later some Black and Tans were moving into the wood to the west of the house. These soldiers approached the house cautiously. Periodically, they halted, lay down, fired and, receiving no answer, advanced closer to the house. The Column held their fire until the Black and Tans were very close. Then the order was given and the Column opened fire. This surprise reply scattered the British. They turned and ran from the hail of bullets, leaving some casualties behind them. The Column moved off towards Clonakilty and the intended attack on Rosscarbery Barracks was postponed to a later date.

Following the success at Crossbarry on 19th March 1921, the Flying Column moved west again and billeted in the Kilmeen Company area. Rosscarbery RIC Barracks was the target again.

While the Column had many great fighting men who were equal to any opposition with rifle or revolver, they had no man capable of making an effective mine. This was vital if they were to successfully take Rosscarbery Barracks. During the stop in the Kilmeen area, a local officer, Tim O'Donoghue, made contact with a Capt McCarthy from the district, who had served as an officer in the Royal Engineers throughout the 1914-1918 war, and who was willing to make a mine and some small canister bombs. The

*The Royal Irish Constabulary Barracks, Rosscarbery which was attacked and destroyed by the West Cork Brigade I.R.A. in April 1921. From the time of this successful operation until the Truce the British were unable to occupy Rosscarbery.*

## The Capture of Rosscarbery RIC Barracks

material for these was got as far away as Berehaven and Crosspound, near Bandon, and brought to the home of John O'Mahony, Ballinvard, where the mine was prepared.

On Wed 30th March 1921, the Column moved into the Reenascreena Company area and was billeted in Cashel and Dunscullib. The headquarters was Whites of Cashel, which is now the Murphy home; and at Noonan's of Dunscullib, now owned by Con Keane. Other members stayed in Tim Collins' house, now occupied by the

O'Sullivan family of Dunscullib. In "Guerilla Days in Ireland" Tom Barry says, the Column billeted in Benduff. This is not correct. My father, Dan O'Callaghan, who was responsible for securing safe billets for the Column said that Cashel and Dunscullib were the townlands where the men stayed before marching to Rosscarbery.

The Flying Column paraded at 9pm and the men were told for the first time, they were to move at midnight to attack Rosscarbery RIC Barracks. General Tom Barry outlined the plan of attack and repeated several times the detailed duties of each Section, so that there would be no misunderstanding of the responsibilities of every man. Three groups of five riflemen each were detailed to cut telegraph wires and block roads, chiefly by felling trees between Rosscarbery and the Garrison towns of Skibbereen, Dunmanway and Clonakilty. The obstructions and wire cutting were to be made at designated places and were to commence precisely at 1am, ten minutes before the opening of the attack. Those groups moved off at 11pm.

The remaining fifty-five members of the Column were given the following orders; ten specially selected officers and men were formed into a storming party. Each of these was given two automatics or revolvers, and their rifles were to be carried slung across their backs. They were to lay the mine and rush the breach after the explosion. The second group of ten riflemen had orders to follow up with improvised torches. The third group of twelve riflemen was to occupy positions north and east of the Barracks and prevent the garrison emerging from the back or side. The fourth group of twelve riflemen was subdivided into three, each with four men to hold the roads in the immediate vicinity of the town. These would prevent the attacking party from being surprised by enemy reinforcements. The fifth group of eleven riflemen was to act as a reserve party, and immediately the attack commenced, they were to open up all the shops that sold petrol and paraffin oil, and fill the fuel into a dozen buckets and half pint bottles. Sonny Maloney and James Hayes of the Rosscarbery Company were given revolvers and were to act as guides. For sometime before this attack, Sonny Maloney had secretly oiled the gate at the entrance to the Barracks, to make sure that it didn't squeak when opened.

The RIC Barracks was on the site of the present Garda Station. The attacking force comprised of twenty-one officers and men. Defending the Barracks were a head constable, two sergeants and nineteen constables.

At midnight, the Column moved off, leaving the quietness of Dunscullib and Cashel, not knowing what lay ahead. They moved south through Reavileen.

From there they marched on, having Benduff on their right side and Froe to their left, then down to Castle Salem and Ardagh. A mile from Rosscarbery, they halted to remove their boots. The mine and bombs were removed from a farm cart and taken by the riflemen.

They entered the town by the new line road, (this is the high road into the town from the west) then through North Square and on to where the Post Office was then, (now Madge Hayes' house) about thirty yards from the Barracks. The mine, which weighed about eighty pounds, was raised on the shoulders of Jack Corkery, Peter Kearney, Tom Kelleher and Christy O'Connell. The fuses were lit and they moved to the Barracks door as quickly as possible. With the mine in position, these men moved out to the footpath and lay there. The mine exploded, but not as they had wished. It blew a hole in the door and the steel shutters off two of the windows. It also did considerable damage to O'Mahony's roof across the road. Rushing into the Barracks, as they had planned, was not an option as the Garrison were firing at their attackers before the dust had settled.

The Column fired some volleys, but because of their location, very few could get into firing positions. Neilus Connolly of Skibbereen and three others were sent to O'Mahony's house across the road, to fire on the Barracks from upstairs. The fight continued using rifles, revolvers and bombs. After two hours, the Garrison retreated upstairs. At this stage the Column used some of its seven-pound charges in the ground floor rooms, to bring down the ceilings, but the upper floors still held. The paraffin and petrol was then thrown into the smouldering building setting the stairs on fire.

The attackers continued to shoot and although the Garrison put up a stubborn defence they were forced into a top storey back room. The end came after four and a half hours fighting. The Column could not get up the stairs because of the flames but neither could the defenders come down to surrender. The Garrison threw all their arms and ammunition on to the burning stairway, lowered their wounded through the back window and climbed down, making their escape to the safety of

## The Capture of Rosscarbery RIC Barracks

the local convent. Nine were wounded; Head Constable Neary; Constables Brady, Woodford, Sullivan, O'Keeffe, Roberts, Doyle, Kinsella and Harken. The bodies of Sergeant Shea and Constable Bowles could not be recovered from the burning building. The Flying Column left the town at daybreak, moving north to billets in the Rossmore area.

General Tom Barry says in his book Guerilla Days In Ireland, "The RIC and Black and Tans, as a force, were detested by the masses of the people and had committed many atrocities in West Cork. This Garrison however had not killed, or wounded, a single citizen nor had they burned houses. They were unique in this respect." For this reason, General Tom Barry did not want to kill any of the Garrison, as he regarded them as decent men. He made it very clear in his book that they only wanted to capture the Barracks, arms and ammunition.

The boundary wall of the old Barracks is still standing between Mrs Madge Hayes' house and the present Garda Station. Some of the stone from the Barracks was used to build the toilets at the Warren strand, and more of the stone was used to improve the old pier near the coastguard station.

The day after the attack was fair day in Ross and, in case of reprisal, the local Volunteers advised people not to go to the fair. Some people may not have got the warning and others may have ignored it. In any case a number of people attended the fair. Among those present were crown forces; one of whom threw a grenade into the crowd, killing two men and injuring several other people. Those killed were Patrick Collins from Derryduff and George Wilson from the townland of Derry. One of those injured was James O'Sullivan of Carrigroe.

On June 26th 1921 a group of more than one hundred auxiliaries arrived in the town. General Tom Barry with thirty-three of the Column, including a small group of local volunteers, attacked these crown forces. In daylight, the Column came down the Ardagh road. One section was sent off to enter the town from the high ground on the west side. The other section moved down the Caim Hill, to enter the town from the east. The planned attack didn't work out as expected. After a brief engagement the Column withdrew. They had done enough to force the auxiliaries to leave town.

*Workers at Pairc A Tobair*

*Catherine and Margaret, weeding and hoeing.*

# Pairc A Tobair

*by Kathy Cunningham*

Why ecology now? Over one hundred and seventy years ago, Catherine McAuley founded the Congregation of the Sisters of Mercy in response to the urgent health care and educational needs of her time. As those needs changed new responses were called for, and this is true in a very radical way in our time. Today the very health of our planet is endangered. We are now realising that humans can survive as a species only if we learn to live in harmony with other species. And so in '98 the Mercy Leadership Team decided to dedicate some Congregational resources - land and personnel - as a gesture in this direction. The Ecology Project in the Convent Field in Rosscarbery is part of this commitment. Kathy and Maria are two of the Sisters who have been assigned to this work. Dominic Waldron was also asked to come on board as a Permaculturist.

Nature is in charge - not us. Our work on the ground at Pairc a Tobair started at the entrance. When we arrived in March 2000 water was gushing out here and we set to work to make this little waterfall a welcoming feature. We wanted to preserve the diversity of growth on the bank and to enhance it by introducing plants that would grow here naturally. Our first and ongoing task was to learn the names of the plants that grow here - the permanent members of the community of life in which we hoped to find our place. We removed the plants that would be too aggressive, briars, bindweed and creeping buttercup, and introduced foxglove and primrose. A good day's work! But a month later the waterfall had dried up and our first plan, like so many that followed, had to be changed.

Less than perfect! But changing plans only requires flexibility and a bit of imagination. More difficult to face are the compromises we have to make. The first and biggest was making a roadway to the site for our potting shed/house. Here was a two-pronged compromise - accommodating fossil-fuel-burning vehicles, and removing soil to do it. Maybe, in time, we will manage without a car but we don't feel ready for that yet.

## PAIRC A TOBAIR

Once upon a time this hillside was covered with woodland. In time the first humans came and hunted and foraged here. Later the woodland was cut down, and the fullacht fiadh and ancient well in the northeast corner of the field testify to a settlement in the area in early agricultural times. One of our reasons for naming the field Pairc a' Tobair was to preserve this memory. In recent years the field has been used for grazing cattle. Chemical fertilisers have killed off many of the soil organisms and the diversity of plant life has been drastically reduced in favour of a monoculture of Italian rye grass. Our task is to allow the soil to recover its own self-nourishing capacity. Reintroducing a variety of plants that would have grown naturally here invites back the insects, which in turn attract the birds and small mammals. Also the roots of the leafy plants grow deep into the earth opening up the soil and restoring its capacity to absorb moisture and air.

## TURNING PROBLEMS INTO SOLUTIONS

On the problem of the removal of the soil we hope that we have somewhat made up for the damage by protecting the soil we removed and using it as a refuge for wild plants and insects. We used the topsoil to make a bank on the southern side of the roadway. This provides shelter for the garden area from the north winds, which sweep across the field, and will provide an area where permacultural food plants, herbs and wildflowers will coexist. We have made a start this year with plum trees, potatoes, fennel, cardoons and other vigorous plants in a mulch of straw.

Multiple functions are a recurrent theme in the permaculture approach. This is well illustrated by the bank on the left side of the road. This bank of subsoil provides shelter from the wind, and a refuge to an increasing diversity of wild plants and their insect associates (valuable as predators in the nearby vegetable garden). It also provides a south facing backdrop reflecting sunlight and storing heat for a herb bed of rich, well drained topsoil at its base.

## HERBS AND HEALING

One of the reasons we want to grow herbs is for their healing properties. Merely walking in their vicinity can restore one's sense of well-being over time. But we hope that Pairc a' Tobair will also have a wider healing dimension. Whether working with the soil, observing the plant and animal life or simply enjoying the beauty of this place, we are deepening our connection with the natural world, restoring inner balance and healing our sense of isolation.

## PERMACULTURE

The permacultural approach encourages us to observe the realities of our home place and to develop ecologically sound strategies while we learn how to fit ourselves back into the landscape and the whole community of life. Two of its themes, which we have already mentioned, are multiple functions and turning problems into solutions.

The planning of paths and roadways is another aspect of permaculture design. At the centre of our path network is the compost area. Here the dying plants, the surplus or the waste organic matter or food are transformed by the micro-organisms into nourishment for next season's growth. How we underestimate bacteria! Less than half a billion years after the formation of the Earth the first bacteria emerged and for the next two billion years bacteria were the only life forms. Then the first plants and animals appeared and it was easy from there on - the bacteria had worked out all the basic life processes.

## TREES

On the southern boundary we have planted a mix of native trees and we intend to continue this planting each year so that native woodland will gradually re-establish around the perimeter - the smaller shrubs and flowers following the trees and inviting the insects, birds and animals, all adding to the richness of the community of life. They also enhance both drainage and water storage in the soil and create sheltered microclimates.

Elsewhere in the field hazel and ash trees have been planted as a renewable source of wood in future years. Their branches can be coppiced at intervals while the trees continue to grow. Increasingly, we intend to meet our needs from sources that are sustainable.

## OUR ECOLOGICAL FOOTPRINT

My "ecological footprint" is the productive land necessary to support my lifestyle. It is a useful idea for thinking about sustainability. There is a limited area of land in the world from which to meet our needs. The goods we use and consume in this country come from all over the world and they all use some of the world's limited productive land. The world has only 1.5 hectares available for each person. Most of the people in Africa use far less than that but we in Ireland have an average "footprint" of 5.9 hectares. Our ecological current account is heavily overdrawn! However living in a more sustainable way does not mean that we cannot enjoy a good life. Here in Pairc a Tobair we find that we can have a much richer life if we live in harmony with nature. But we have to pay attention to what we use, how it is produced, and if there is exploitation of people, other animals or land in its production or transport.

## FOOD AND COMMUNITY

The nucleus garden provides us with much of our food. Some of this is produced in the deep beds, which are planted in a three-year rotation of legumes, roots and leaves. But much of it comes from plants, which self seed and grow wherever the seed falls. The diversity, which does so much for the health of the land, also enhances human health providing a range of nutrients, which our bodies have learnt to assimilate as they evolved in this bioregion. But in feeding our bodies we also feed our souls. Sharing of food is a symbol of communion between people in all cultures and it is also a symbol and an expression of our communion with all of life. We recall this gift of communion in our grace before meals:

*"From air and soil, from bees and sun,*
*From others' toil, my bread is won ...................*
*So I must think each day afresh*
*How food and drink became my flesh......................" (B. K. Mason)*

We try to bring to our planting, tending, harvesting, cooking and eating the reverence that belongs to a sacred activity.

### HERITAGE SEEDS

Around the nucleus garden we have planted a circle of apple trees, which we hope will form a natural shelterbelt in time. It will then replace the plastic mesh (or the green circle), which is the field's most visible feature at present. Inside the garden we have also planted eighteen varieties of old Irish apple trees. With so much standardisation and control of seeds by multinational companies the variety, which is the hallmark of a vigorous, healthy food supply is being eroded. We have become active members of Irish Seed Savers Association, one of the groups working to protect our food heritage.

### THE UNIVERSE STORY

Recalling our origin story from the initial flaring forth - through the formation of the first stars, of planet Earth, the bacteria, fish, ferns, insects, birds, trees, humans and bears - fills us with a deep sense of wonder and mystery, of gratitude and responsibility. All our activities are inspired in some way by this mystery but in order to focus on it explicitly we are developing a meditation garden at the top of the field marking some of these stages in our evolution.

### THE HUMAN DIMENSION OF PAIRC A TOBAIR

We have been blessed in our helpers in the garden - John with his building experience and his broad knowledge and feel for the land; Jeremiah with his keen interest in integrating ecology with the best of traditional agriculture. Declan with his enthusiasm for new ideas and his ability to turn his hand to so many things; Noel, a powerful digger, with his ecological mode of transport; and John S., with his knowledge of the area, his good humour and love of the land. Then Cathal arrived and discovered a

*Photo Gallery* **77**

*Lisavaird First Communion: l to r: Fr. P. Walshe, Michael Denis Santry, Laura Deasy, Emma Kingston, Seamus Whyte, Kathleen Eady (Teacher)*

*Ardagh Boys First Communion 19-5-01. Left to right, Christopher O'Donovan, Peter White, Kevin O'Neill, Cian O'Mahony, Terry O'Donovan, Bobby Kelly, Thomas Jennings, Alan O'Regan, David Flavin.*

*Scenes from Pairc a Tobair: clockwise from left, Dominic and Paddy discussing the mulberries. Claire Watson; Dolores contemplates lunch!; assembling the "second hand" house with Michael Harte in foreground; Jeremiah, Josie, Declan and John O'Donovan arriving with sea-weed.*

*Photo Gallery*

*Rosscarbery Girls: front row l to r: Mrs Fiona Deasy (teacher), Laura Hodnett, Aisling O'Sullivan, Sinead Dalton, Zena O'Reilly, Sorcha Kelly, Triona Hayes, Zena O'Driscoll, Mary-Rose O'Brien, Sarah O'Mahony, Bishop John Buckley. Back row l to r: Sr. Redempta, Orla O'Mahony, Johanna O'Sullivan, Saidhbh Hyland, Emma Fitzpatrick, Laura White, Jennifer Connolly, Margaret Hayes, Elaine O'Sullivan, Katie Hodnett.*

*Rosscarbery Boys, front l to r: Michael Cussen, David O'Regan, Kevin O'Sullivan, Daniel Kelly, Brian Hayes, Shane Coggin, Kevin Draper, Damien O'Halloran, Eamonn Gallagher, Stephen Coakley, Killiam Moloney, Liam Anthony. Back row l to r: James Hicks (Teacher), Andrew O'Sullivan, Killean Reardon, Eoin O'Mahony, David Hayes, Gerard O'Mahony, Aidan Walsh, Daniel Nagle, James Nagle, Barry Murphy, Micheal O'Sullivan, Daniel White.*

*Photo Gallery*

*U-14 B West Cork champions, back row left to right, Eoin O'Mahony, Martin Collins, Brian Shannon, Eoin O'Gorman, James Fitzpatrick, James Cussen, Ciarian O'Brien, Sean Dignan, Daniel Nagle, Kevin Sheehy, Jeremy Nagle. Front row, l. to r., Sam Dignan, Daniel Kelly, Michael Mennis, Micheal Kelly, Brian Hayes, Myles O'Riordan, Michael Cussen, Killian O'Riordan, Nicholas Peters.*

*Mount St. Michael junior footballers: back row l to r: John O'Donovan, Liam Harte, Sean Dignan, Anthony Coakley, Fachtna Fitzpatrick, Daniel O'Donovan, Stephen Hicks (Captain) Kieran O'Donovan, Paul O'Driscoll, Niall McCarthy, Conor Ryan, Mike Keohane (Coach). Front row l to r: Frank Hayes, Sean O'Driscoll, Ryan Hourihane, Stephen Kearns, Micheal Kelly James Fitzpatrick, Jeremy Nagle, James Cussen, Brian Shanahan*

*Reenascreena Confirmation, back row l to r; Vincent Dullea (teacher), Deirdre O'Donovan, Laura McCarthy, Michael Mennis, Denise Ronan, Sinead O'Brien, Kevin Sheehy, Claire O'Regan. Front row l to r: Ann Kearns (teacher) Rosarie Collins, Elaine Lawlor, Christina Collins, Maire O'Brien, Mary Connolly, James Whyte, Daniel Collins, Louise McCarthy, Bishop John Buckley.*

*Rosscarbery First Communion: l to r: Karen O'Sullivan Eilis White, Adele Gallwey, Catherine Walsh, Aoife Goggin, Roisin Vickery, Tara Maguire, Louise O'Donovan, Assumpta Hayes, Anne Marie O'Neill, Rachel Dempsey, Edel Hayes, Amy Jennings.*

Photo Gallery 83

*Lisavaird Confirmation: back row l to r: Patrick French (Principal), Patrick Deasy, Helen Barry, Amy O'Gorman, Michelle Whyte, Eimear Brennan. Front row l to r: Edel Calnan, David Kingston, Gemma Whyte, Fearghal Beamish, Gerard McCarthy, Callaghan McCarthy, Barry McCarthy, John O'Dowd, Colin O'Brien, Bishop John Buckley.*

*Reenascreena First Communion: back row l to r: Stephen O'Connor, Ian Ronan, Micheal O'Donovan. Front row l to r: Michelle Lawlor, Eilis Collins, Cait Mennis, Avril O'Driscoll, Ann Kearns (Teacher).*

*U14 Girtls football: back l to r: Orla Crowley, Jennifer Hourihane, Therese Keohane, Louise Nyhan, Donna Hayes, Amanda Jennings, Brid O'Donovan, Sinead O'Brien, Elaine Whooley, Angela Collins, Margaret Hayes, Kate O'Brien, Jenny Dineen, Emma Fitzpatrick. Front l to r: Margaret Coone, Adele Jennings, Laura McMahon, Karen Collins, Orla Crowley, Sinead O'Regan, Eilish O'Donovan, Trina Hayes, Deirdre Hayes, Maura O'Brien, Catriona O'Mahony*

*Scor Na Bpaisti: West Cork Finalists: front l to r: Clare O'Regan, Rosarie Collins, Denise Collins, Katrina O'Driscoll. Back l to r: Deirdre O'Donovan, Kate Dodnett, Cristine Collins and Lena O'Driscoll*

*Pairc A Tobair*

latent talent for stonework. As well as providing boundaries that are both beautiful and practical the stones also provide a niche for shelter loving plants and animals - including the beetles, which eat the slugs, which would otherwise eat our lettuces! Josie brings with her a fund of wisdom and a holistic approach to life encompassing plants and food, cures and cooking. Dolores and Margaret, two of our Mercy colleagues with a background in theology, have a keen interest in developing a spirituality, which is rooted in the soil, embraces all of life and is inspired by the new universe story. And Catherine is working on the musical and educational dimension of the project. But ninety per cent of the work that has been done would never have got started if it weren't for Sean - finding and organising competent workers, and maintaining a constant interest in the venture.

Our Committee members, Bernie, Marcella, Dominic, and Sandra have been a source of guidance, inspiration and support from the very beginning. To add to this Clare brings her facilitative skills and her experience as an organic gardener, all this helping us focus and clarify our direction.

From the start Donal Harte's contribution to the project has been huge. His advice around building and his constant support saw us through our first winter here. Paddy O Donovan, with his sense of ecology and local history, keeps reminding us of the wider picture.

### STUDY GROUP

A Study Group also meets here on a regular basis. It provides a space for looking at the disturbing issues of our time and for exploring wider dimensions such as Cosmology, meaning and spirituality.

### DIVERSIFY OR DIE

The story of the evolution of the universe is one of increasing complexity and diversity. There have been millions of crises in the unfolding story but the way forward has always been through increased diversity. One of the temptations to which we humans are prone is to oversimplify - to reduce diversity to uniformity. Some of us are more prone to this than others - especially if we think in straight lines and have no previous experience of gardening! It would seem so much easier to plant what we want and eliminate everything else! But the story of our evolution tells us that to diversify is our nature. We are all endlessly creative! So we are slowly getting to know the other life forms in our little plot of land. But to know our own bit we must know the context. So we also want to study our bioregion in all its magnificence and diversity - its rocks and waterways, its plants, animals and birds and our place within the symphony of life. For this learning we hope to draw on the expertise of the geographers, geologists, biologists, historians and nature lovers of the area.

## THE GOOD LIFE!

One of the things we love about being here is the simplicity of the life and the fact that it is all of a piece. There is something unifying about picking vegetables for dinner from the garden after a morning's work there, or stepping outside the door for morning prayer at sunrise. And for all of this, we're still nuns at heart - we enjoy our visits to the local convents - Clon, Ross, Skibb and Bantry - where we both have connections from our earliest days in Convent life.

## A PLACE OF LEARNING

We hope that Pairc a Tobair will become a place of learning for those who want to relate with the earth in a new way. In this field no one knows it all but everyone has her/his wisdom to offer - we are all members of the earth community. And the earth is our first and greatest teacher.

Some comments from the team at Pairc a Tobair:

*"Tis a good experience working here with the other people...learning about organic gardening, planting and mulching trees and minding them." (Noel)*

*"Working here brings me a kind of stability.... there was something missing in my life...this gives a bit of meaning to things...I find myself whistling coming to work in the morning."(John S.)*

*"Coming from a city environment, this here gives a balance...learning about a sustainable way of living and not damaging the environment or myself."(Cathal)*

*"It can only be a good thing to produce things without chemicals or pesticides, and then to see how all things work together for the good of the whole." (Jeremiah)*

*"Working in Parc a Tobair I can describe in one word "Tranquility""(Declan)*

*"We are so happy here with our workmates and sisters learning about organic gardening as we have never done before and finding that it all works" (John O'D)*

# Sand Dredging in Leap

*by John French*

In the first half of the 20th century the use of sea sand as a source of lime for the soil was a very common practice. Barley, sugar beet, grass and clover etc would not thrive without it.

In Clonakilty and Rosscarbery the sand was shored when the tide was out but in the Leap, Glandore and Union Hall areas the sand had to be dredged, which meant the sand had to be collected when the tide was out but even then it had to be taken out of many feet of water.

To promote the use of sand the County Committee of Agriculture gave an incentive to the farmers, i.e. the farmer had to take two boat loads and the Committee would pay for one. Four sand boats operated out of Leap, John O'Donovan, The Quay, and John Calnan each had one boat and T O'Donovan & Sons had two boats. There were always four men on each boat and the price of the sand was divided five ways – one share for the boat and the remainder for the men.

The sand was collected off Carrigillihy and had to be pulled all the way up to the quay in Leap by four oarsmen. They went out with the tide, loaded their boats and came in with the next tide.

The dredge was an implement made by the blacksmith, it was an 8ft strip of flat iron 8 inches wide and _ inch thick, turned into a half circle, a line of holes was drilled 6in apart along one side and the other side beaten out thin to make a blade. At right angles to that, on the blade side, two heavy bars of iron were attached, each was 4ft long and they were bent until they met at the far end. They were welded together and an eye put in to attach the steel rope from the boat. On the row of holes there was a heavy jute bag attached and that was the dredge complete.

On the boat there was a winch, a derrick and a steel rope. On top of the derrick there was a pulley, the steel rope went from the winch over the pulley and on to the dredge. The dredge was thrown out – the boat was moved back and held with the anchor, the four men went on the winch, two on either side and dragged the dredge along the bed of the sea until the bag was full. They continued pulling until the bag came in over the front of the boat. Then they manhandled the bag, turned it upside down to empty it and repeated the performance until their load was full, which could amount to eighteen to twenty tons of wet sand.

Then the long haul to Leap Quay where the boat was unloaded by the four men using hand shovels, onto a quay that was often three to four feet higher than the boat. Their wage out of each load would amount to about six shillings (30p)

None of those men are still with us. A few names that come to mind are Mike O'Donoghue (Tim John's father), McCarthys, Aughatuba, O'Regans and Hegartys, Curraheen, Leap, Daly brothers, Maulagow, O'Sullivan brothers, Droum, Mike Hamilton, Droum, John Hurley, The Quay.

There was one problem with collecting the subsidy – the sand had to be drawn before 31st December so the pressure was on. On one occasion, the day after St. Stephen's Day, T. O'Donovan woke to find eight farmers from Drimoleague parish knocking at his door to get the form signed to collect the subsidy. He approached them calmly saying "Be Jesus lads 'tis worse than the Easter duty with ye, ye never think of these things until the last minute ".

The sand was drawn by horses as far as Drimoleague and north as far as Kilronan. Names that come to mind are Willie Whinnie O'Regan, Drinagh Steeple; Bob Ellis, Cur-

*John Calnan's sandboat in front of his house at Sunnycove, Leap*

raghalickey; Con Dan (na Habhan) O'Driscoll, Derryclough; O'Donovans and McCarthys, Drominidy and Rerahanagh; The Goods and O'Driscolls, Kilskohonagh and many more.

The farmers further north, around Dunmanway, went to Castlemore where they got burned lime. It was troublesome, messy and hard to spread.

This type of work is history now. Ground limestone replaced sea sand and burned lime in the early 1950's. This limestone was subsidised by money given by the USA, known as Marshal Aid. Now we have lorries for transporting and machinery of every type for spreading lime, which makes life on the land much easier.

Extract from Cork Committee of Agriculture Annual Report
*Lime and Sea-Sand schemes 1946-47*
*The following are particulars of the amount of money allocated and some of the principal conditions of these schemes:*
*Amount allocated by the County Committee of Agriculture - £8000*
*Amount allocated by the Department of Agriculture - £11000*
*Rate subsidy for Lime:-*
*For persons not more than ten miles from the nearest kiln - 1/6 per barrel*
*For persons over ten miles from the nearest kiln - 1/9 per barrel*
*Maximum quantity of lime subsidised - 36 barrels*
*Rate of subsidy for Sea Sand - 3/- per ton*
*Maximum quantity of sea sand subsidised - 18 tons*
*Number of lime kilns 25*
*Number of sand boats 52*
*Total number of applications for Lime Subsidy 4500*
*Total number of applications for Seas Sand Subsidy 3940*
*The regulations governing this scheme require that the lime and sea sand be drawn not later than 31st December each year. A very large number of applicants lose the benefit of the subsidy by failing to obtain delivery within the specified period. It is hoped that in future they will make every effort to order their requirements and get deliveries in time.*

# Afternoon

*by Eugene Daly*

Lying on the lichened rocks
at Owenahincha, I see waves
dancing in the summer sun
like fish scales or silver sixpences

I rise and stroll along the strand
until I reach a rock-pool
where green crabs scuttle sideways
into the cover of doolamaun.

At my feet a scurry of wave-drawn pebbles.
Curlews rise in a tumult of wings and cries.
A slow wave washes the smooth stones
in a hundred wondering whispers.

I cover my eyes from the blaze
of the westering sun. Melodies
of sea-sound echo on the skerries.
I am enveloped in endless blue light.

# The Importance of Children and Young People

*by Catherine (Kay) Wheeler*

Since coming to live in Roury Glen, Rosscarbery, I have had the good fortune and immense pleasure of being involved with the children and young people of Rosscarbery and the surrounding area through craft work. The reason I thought of writing this article is so that you, too, may have the pleasure of seeing and knowing of all the marvellous work in the area of arts and crafts that is being done by so many children and young people in and around Rosscarbery.

I have been mounting displays of the students' art and craft work in the Convent for the annual Art & Literature Festival. Due to the wonderful work done by the students for the Festival, this year one of them, a 6th year students at Mount St Michael, Kevin Tuohy, who had done several sculptures, sold two pieces of his work. Indeed there was a lot of interest from people wanting to know if other pieces of artwork were also for sale.

The first year students at Mount St Michael's had produced a life-size banner of a disco scene. This was displayed in the Celtic Ross Hotel during the festival and was later awarded a prize by UCC. Second year students made posters based on a lecture they had had on the origins of Rosscarbery. These were entered in a competition and the winners were: 1st Lisa Gallwey, 2nd Clare O'Regan, and 3rd Joseph Peglar.

Of the younger children the boys and girls of the local National Schools entered an art competition for the Festival, this involved poetry, stories and paintings. The winners were Bobby Kelly and David O'Regan from the boys' school and Karen O'Sullivan, Aine Kelly, Megan O'Riordan and Tara Maguire from the girls' school. There were also exhibits from Rathbarry School of some marvellous artwork done by the students there.

I am also involved, with Sara Hodson and Mim Hill, in the running of an Arts and Crafts Class for children from five to twelve years. Fiona O'Donovan, who comes every Saturday morning to help us bring out the magic that all children have hidden within them, is a valued member of our team

Leading up to this year's Festival

*Kay Fitzgerald (Granny Kay) with entrants in the Poster Competition*

*1 left: Sorcha Kelly, Alan O'Regan, Bobby Kelly, Eileen McCarthy, Eoin Kelly and Philip Bendon*
*right: Orla Kelly, Laura Hill, Eimear Hayes and Michael McCarthy*

*The Importance of Children*

we had the children make mosaics, which were displayed in The Square during the Festival. There were six works in total, two of which were sold.

One day, when preparing displays for the Festival, I was shown around the Convent School by Sr. Angela. I saw some magnificent work done by students from the metal and woodwork classes there. This work was all of a very high standard and worthy of display. It was a shame to see this talent hidden away in a classroom.

All this goes to show the high quality of work that children and young people can achieve if given the encouragement

*Above, left: Shannon Hill Susan Dempsey, Ruth Nagle, Fiona Nagle, and Cliona Maguire. Right: Ciara McDonald, Eimear O'Rourke, Marie Jennings and Oilbhe O'Callaghan*
*Below, left: Katie O'Reilly, Orla Hodnett, Rachel Dempsey, Sadhbh O'Callaghan and Katie O'Donovan, Tara Maguire. Right: Peter White, Elizabeth White, Aoife McDonald, Collette Galway and Ann Nyman*

Threshing at Denis Cullinane's, Bohonagh, 1954. Back left to right, Joe O'Sullivan, Michael Lane, Dan Fitzpatrick, John Fitzpatrick, Jimmy O'Sullivan, Sheila Cullinane, Paddy Scully, Danny A. O'Regan, Ger Sweeney on tractor.

# The Drowning

*by Kevin Murphy*

The 15th of July 2001 marked the 40th anniversary of one of the saddest tragedies ever to occur in the locality when three of our, then, very young friends, Ann Wilson, Robert Kelly and Brian Bodden, lost their lives in what became known locally as The Drowning.

The Ross Carnival was to begin the next day and six of us: Brian Bodden, Anthony Calnan, Robert Kelly, Tony Murphy, Alan Wilson, and myself, high-spiritedly made our way to the bridge on a chilly mid-July evening. Our intention was to put to sea in that 10' flat bottomed boat which had been lying at the water's edge on English Island (opposite where the Celtic Ross Hotel now stands) for some time. En route we were joined by Ann Wilson and Thelma O'Regan who pleaded with us to allow them to partake in the adventure.

Initially, all eight of us boarded the boat and, with no oars at our disposal, we improvised by using two long poles to push the boat out on the full tide that was just beginning to ebb. The thrill of it all was so great that we paid little or no heed to the fact that the boat was taking in water and that all of us were non-swimmers. The excitement mounted as we moved away from the shore. The sense of adventure increased as, here we were, about to emulate the seafaring feats of some of our weekly comic heroes.

In the excitement Tony had boarded with his footwear on. Shortly his feet were immersed in water, which necessitated a successful return to dry land. Buoyed up by this accomplished manoeuvre we headed out to sea again, this time more daring and with increased confidence but unfortunately we were not destined to make another safe return to shore.

All was well and relaxed while the poles succeeded in making contact with the seabed but then panic set in as the boat continued to fill with water and we found ourselves drifting seawards on the ebbing tide. The water was becoming deeper and we were unable to utilise the poles to propel ourselves back towards the shore. By this time Tony understood the gravity of the situation and ran to the Square to summon help. Our screams were raised and continued

*Tony Murphy, Finbarr Hennessy, Lawrence Murphy and Brian Calnan with the ill-fated boat (15th July 1961).
Photo Courtesy of Liam Kennedy, Strawberry Beds, Dublin 20*

unabated. Jumpers were tied to the poles and frantically waved in the air in order to draw attention to our plight. Some passing motorists did slow down but, to our frustration and disbelief, responded by waving back at us, quite obviously misinterpreting our gestures and screams.

One of the first to hear our cries was Miss Smyth, who lived with her father in a caravan directly across the road from the scene of the tragedy. At first she paid little attention as, a few days previously, she had heard similar cries which turned out to be hoaxes. However, because of the intensity and persistence of our screams, she did investigate after a short time and subsequently ran for help. The next to arrive on the scene were the late Mr and Mrs Paudie O'Brien, both natives of Ross but residents of Cork City, who stopped their car on seeing our predicament and who did their utmost to pacify us. Paudie sped off to the Square for help while Mrs. O'Brien stayed and continued her endeavours to get us to remain still. As old heads cannot be placed on young shoulders all of us instinctively went to the landward side of the boat whereupon it immediately capsized, catapulting us into the sea, the depth of which was almost twice our height.

The rescue operation began with the arrival of three local lads, all in their mid to late teens;

Finbarr Hennessy, Anthony's brother Brian and my brother Laurence, who had previously successfully completed a lifesaving course. They entered the water fully clothed and swam to the overturned boat, upon which they placed those of us fortunate enough to be saved. Two men, James O'Mahony and Tom McCarthy, in a passing CIE lorry, stopped and assisted in the rescue operation. Tom tied a rope around his waist and waded and swam out to the scene. By now Alan was sitting on the upturned boat and Thelma had been saved. The buoyancy of a rubber ball in Robert's blazer pocket aided his rescue. The five of us were hauled ashore on the upturned boat. Artificial respiration was administered to those of us who needed it but unfortunately Robert failed to respond.

In the ensuing confusion one of the difficulties was to determine how many had been in the boat and, consequently, the bodies of Ann and Brian were not recovered until later.

The four of us lucky enough to have been rescued were brought to our respective homes, but our three friends who didn't make it were brought in the opposite direction to Clonakilty hospital. For them life's journey had indeed been short.

Nightfall was accompanied by an eerie silence and a pall of gloom as the stunned local community tried to comprehend, and to come to terms with, the terrible events of the evening. The town, which had been in festive mood, was now in deep mourning and of course the 1961

Carnival was cancelled.

A drowning tragedy in Eanach Dhúin on the banks of Lock Corrib in 1828 inspired the Mayo poet Antaine Ó Raifteirí to compose his well-known lament for those who lost their lives in that accident. The following are the opening lines of the lament, which have the same relevance for Ross as for Eanach Dhúin:

"*Má fhaighimse sláinte beidh caint is tráchtadh
ar an méid a báthadh as Eanach Dhúin
's mo thrua amárach gach athair is máthair,
bean is páiste 'tá ag sileadh súl.*"

*Gaisce silver award winners from Mount St. Michael School, left to right, Peter Hourihane, Jenny Shanahan, Anna McCarthy, Mairead Cadogan, Roberta Jennings, Emer Leonard, Peter O'Donovan, Eoin Milner and president award leader, Yvette Jennings.*

# The Sweeney

*by Joe McSweeney*

The Sweeney or McSweeney names have been associated with the Warren Road, Rosscarbery, for many generations. They all resided in that area and it was often referred to as The Sweeney Hole.

Mick Sweeney, his brothers Johnny, Dan, Patrick (Pat) and his sisters Nancy, Margaret, Katharine, Hannah (Sheila), and possibly others, resided at the Warren Road. Their father was Daniel McSweeney.

Patrick, or Pat, was known as The Captain, probably due to his maritime knowledge. He had a sail ship – a cargo boat type schooner, or cutter, named the Damsel and he worked this boat between the West Cork ports from Kinsale to Glandore and on the north coast of Wales from Milford Haven to Newport.

Tragedy befell the Captain when, on a trip to Union Hall in the 1920's, his son Pat lost his life in an unfortunate accident. He apparently went ashore and on his return to the boat he must have slipped or missed his footing and fell into the water. He got stuck in the heavy mud and with the incoming tide he lost his life.

Mick Sweeney was always involved in boats and fishing and particularly net fishing for mullet, bass and the odd sea trout. He fished from Ross Bar, Bridge Hole and at Owenahincha Strand. Mick's brother Johnny usually sold the fish for him in various locations around the area.

The Warren area was noted for its abundance of sand eel fishing bait. This bait was used by fishermen from far and near along the South West Cork coastline for line and spiller fishing. The local McSweeney and Nagle families were noted for their skills in this type of fishing. They used sand eel size nets specially for this work and the nets were usually set and hauled at either High Tide or Low Water. They were generally set near the Old Coastguard Station, or Fish House, on the Pier Road.

Mick provided the flag boat for every Regatta held in Ross for well over 50 years. This flag boat, along with other boats, was secured in the winter on the small strand inlet near Mick's own house. Alas the sands have completely closed off the channel to that area now.

Their sister Hannah (Sheila) mar-

100                                              *Rosscarbery - Past & Present*

*Mick and Tim Sweeney waiting for the tide near Rosscarbery Bridge, circa 1932*

*Fishing for mullet and bass*

ried John Hickens from Wales on 23rd September 1897. John was a master mariner with the British Merchant Navy. He sailed and traded in the ports of India, Burma, Hong Kong and Eastern Asia. His wife sailed with him and their daughter, Sheila, was born on one of these trips abroad. John Hickens died whilst on one of his voyages and was buried at sea. His wife and daughter set up a Bed and Breakfast house and a small shop in Youghal. When the mother died she was buried in the family grave in Ross Abbey.

The daughter went to live in Cardiff and was employed as a telephonist in the Government Security Department. She later returned to live in Youghal and used to spend many long periods with the O'Keeffe family at their guesthouse in Skibbereen Road. She died in 1996 and is buried with her mother and other Sweeney family members in Ross Abbey.

Other Sweeney families lived on the Warren Road. They were Timothy, Patrick and Dan, three brothers. Their sister, Julia, married and lived in Benduff, Barley Hill. She was the mother of Joe and Johnny Tobin of GAA fame. Incidentally, Mick Sweeney was also a good football player and was on many Ross Rangers teams, including the 1912 Champions team.

All the Sweeney families were fishermen by trade and for generations built their own boats with whatever resources they had, which were very little. They did all types of labouring work to supplement their income, including breaking stones on the roadside. They also met coal boats coming into Rosscarbery to pilot them in. They used to travel as far as the Old Head of Kinsale to try and get the pilot job and this often entailed being out at sea for days on end in all types of weather. Such was their lives in those days.

The call of the sea had many sad tales for so many families in West Cork. Certainly the Rosscarbery area paid a very high price when so many local young men joined the British Navy and, unfortunately, never returned. Jim McSweeney from the Warren Road was one of those. He lost his life in the Mediterranean Sea off Tripoli when the cruiser Neptune was sunk by enemy mines with a loss of 549 out of 550 crew on 3rd January 1941.

Many other locals including sailors from the Galley Head, Rosscarbery, Downeen, Millcove, Ardagh and Glandore areas also perished in those wars and the only consolation their families got was a letter from Buckingham Palace which offered the heartfelt sympathy of King George VI and the Queen for lives so nobly given in the service of England.

The families who were born and grew up along the Warren Road know quite well the damage that was inflicted on the Warren Strand

and local sand dunes for many years by the mountainous seas and winter storms that lashed the area. The present shoreline has moved back by at least 40 metres in the past 70 years. Unless urgent remedial works are carried out, untold and irreparable damage will have been done to the Warren and its sand dunes. Delays to the remedial works have been further compounded by the now infamous Lathyrus Japonicus, or Sea Pea, which is statutorily protected under the Flora (Protection) Order of 1999. The shoreline continues to deteriorate while the powers that be endeavour to reach a satisfactory conclusion and make up their minds to have the problems dealt with because neither time nor tide awaits any man and soon this wonderful amenity at the Warren will be destroyed for ever.

*Jane Scully, at Limbo Horse and Pony Show, presenting a trophy for Champion Brood Mare to James Gorman, Froe, Rosscarbery.*

# The Big Fair

*by Thaddeus O'Regan*

Every child should have a skylight in his room. I slept beneath one as a boy and often woke early to watch the tumbling clouds, the occasional bird drift purposefully past. The skylight was always partially open and sounds swirled in to accompany my skyscape; the rattle of milk churns, Jimmy Keohane chatting to his pony, my father's distinctive walk. These were but solo airs compared to the symphony that flooded my room on 26 August, the day of The Big Fair. It glanced off the sheeting-boards of my ceiling and swirled into my waking mind. It was as if I had gone to sleep in a house and woken up in a wagon on the Steppes of Central Asia. Horses whinnied and snorted, hooves clattered and danced, skidding and scraping on the roadway. All this equine noise was choreographed by owners and buyers doing deals beneath my bedroom window. "Hup our dat...aisy, aisy." "A grand bit of flesh entirely"

I sprang to the skylight and dressed, still standing on the bed. Wide-eyed, I stared at the transformation that had overtaken the town while I slept. A stream of swaying horses cascaded down Ceim Hill and on to the main street, itself a roaring torrent of horseflesh. I ran to our front gate, still marvelling at how the usual small-town atmosphere had been so effectively erased. Strange faces mingled with the locals. Everywhere horses were slapped, patted and, if space could be found, given a little run to show their condition to the vigilant buyers, distinctive in bowler hats, tweeds and white riding coats. They wore burnished, brown Chelsea boots and, oblivious to the increasing piles of horse dung, they strode and stroked, bantered and bargained, slapping hands when the deal was done.

All this was taller than me as a child. I could have walked beneath the bellies of the horses and often narrowly escaped a drenching from spontaneous surges of steaming urine. I peered into pens of squealing bonhams and stared at the people who flowed in and out of the pubs, with glasses in hand celebrating deals and revelling in the day out. Country children, allocated some part of their parents' bounty, bought lemonade and ice cream, while 'townies' tried to locate long-lost blood ties with this new-found affluence. We were all cousins for a day.

In the centre of the town square a few huxters plied their wares. Collectively known as 'Chape Jack' they sold a bit of everything, much of it imported from bazaars farther east – in Hong Kong or Taiwan. 'Genuine' scent, from the Rue de Rivoli, jostled for space with socket sets and chisels. Boots, shoes, plastic toys and thick country socks were festooned from the awnings and stroked my young head as I passed by.

There was always a fight. The fair was incomplete without one. Fuelled by celebratory alcohol, some disagreement would spill out into open tribal conflict. Punches were thrown, insults hurled, an eruption of violence briefly surged, until the Guards stemmed this flow and dragged the chief protagonists to the Barracks, followed by a straggle of staring children. Finally, in the early evening, as the horses were loaded into lorries, 'Paddy Piady' would emerge from a pub. Stripped to the waist and wielding a long whip he balanced chairs on his chin and challenged the onlookers to provide a volunteer who would hold a rolled newspaper in his hand while Paddy cut it in half with the whip.

At sundown I was summoned home. Most of the crowd had departed. The rest were now in the pubs, from which lively singing leaked into the night air. The sights and sounds of the day swirled in my head and mixed with the taste of lemonade and clove rock. I drifted to sleep, knowing that the summer was now really over. In a week we would be back at school.

# Paul Daly - Stonemason

*by Fachtna O'Callaghan*

Paul Daly was born into a farming family in Dromilihy, Leap on 6th April 1859. His parents, Paul Daly and Margaret O'Sullivan had five other children; John, Elizabeth, Margaret and twins William and Seán. Margaret became Mrs. Dan Keohane, Kilfinnan, Glandore.

When he was 17 or 18 years of age Paul emigrated to the U.S. He left Dromilihy and walked to the railway station in Dunmanway (his boots over his shoulder to save the leather). He boarded the train to Queenstown (Cobh) from where he took passage on a sailing ship which reached New York six weeks later.

In New York he worked with John Walsh, a large builder from Queenstown (Cobh) and became a very skilled builder and stonemason. Over the next 30-40 years he worked intermittently in the U.S. and at home, making seven trips in all to the U.S. He worked on major construction jobs there, including the Brooklyn Bridge in New York.

Records at Ellis Island show two of the trips that he made to the U.S.A. In 1904 he sailed from Queenstown on the steamer Campania. On the ship's manifest it shows that he was interested in taking out American citizenship. He went to Philadelphia, Pennsylvania, where records show that he had been to the city on an earlier trip to America.

His next visit was in 1906. This time he sailed on the Caronia and was registered as a U.S. citizen.

An example of his work locally is the porch on Leap Parish Church, which he built about 1900. There are also examples of his stonework on the family farm in Dromilihy.

When Kilfaughtnabeg Church (Glandore) was being built in 1927-29 Paul acted as Clerk of Works as he did for the Union Hall church, 1930-32, and Clonakilty Technical School, 1933-34. The building contractor for all three was a Mr Coffey from Midleton.

At this stage he would have been 74 but no early retirement for Paul Daly as his skills were in demand and he continued to work locally. He did much work on the four big houses in Glandore. He worked on Glandore House, later the Convent, for Judge Cohalan; on West View, now Greenstone Hall, for Robert Travers;

*The Caronia* (Photo Alex Dunan, Albert Wilhelmi Collection)

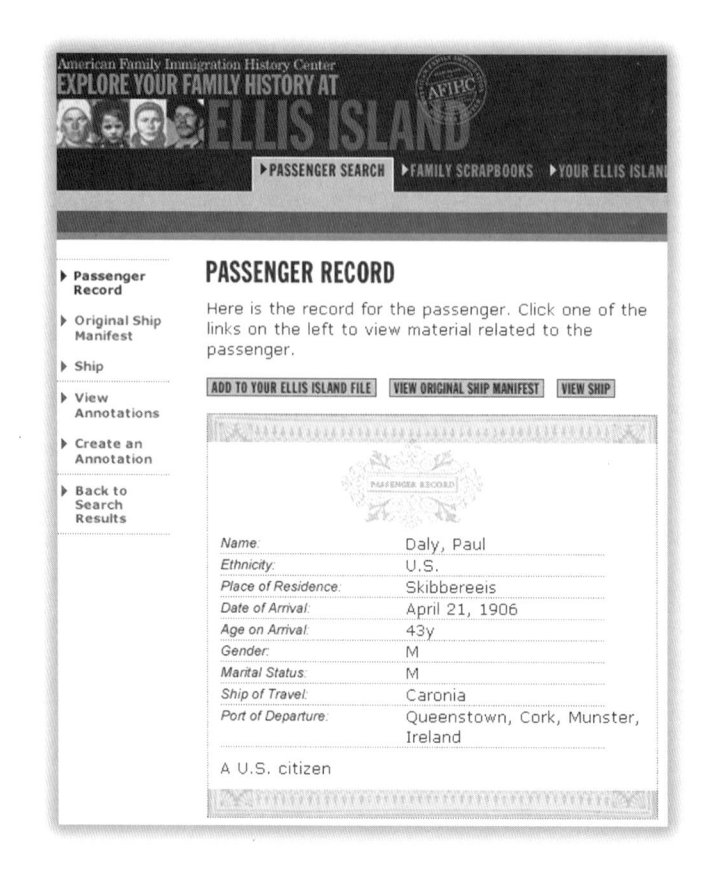

**PASSENGER RECORD**

Here is the record for the passenger. Click one of the links on the left to view material related to the passenger.

| | |
|---|---|
| Name: | Daly, Paul |
| Ethnicity: | U.S. |
| Place of Residence: | Skibbereeis |
| Date of Arrival: | April 21, 1906 |
| Age on Arrival: | 43y |
| Gender: | M |
| Marital Status: | M |
| Ship of Travel: | Caronia |
| Port of Departure: | Queenstown, Cork, Munster, Ireland |

A U.S. citizen

on Stonehall for Dr. Welply and on East View, now the Rectory, for Rev. John Boardman.

Paul married Julia O'Donovan of Clounties in 1898 and had seven in family, four boys and three girls. His son, Paul Daly of Leap, carried on the building tradition in the next generation although he was probably better known as a plumber.

Paul Snr. died in 1945 after a long and productive life leaving many memorials in stone.

### ACKNOWLEDGEMENT:

My thanks to Paul's son Peter Daly, Droumilihy, and his granddaughter, Frances Harrington of Leap, who supplied material for this article.

*The Porch at Leap Chapel.*

*The Rosscarbery under 16 boys crew who won their grade at the county yaul rowing finals at Union Hall recently. Back from left- Chris Hayes, Colin Crowley, David Jennings, Mark O'Callaghan and at front Vincent Harte, cox. (photo- Tom Newman).*

# The History of Trotting

*by Jackie Cowan*

## PART 1

Around the turn of the last century trotting races were regularly held in conjunction with flat and jump events, and often bicycle races too.

On St Stephen's Day 1899 three trotting races were held on the road in Durrus, with the sports taking place in a field. The Open Trot was won by Jeremiah Nugent, Dunbeacon, while the Parish, in which six ran, went to Michael Hegarty, Dooneen. First prize was £1 and second a double bridle. On the same day a steeplechase and two trotting matches were run at Drinagh, along with sports. One of the trotting races was won by M. McCarthy, R.D.C., Drominidy who made the pace for all comers and was an easy winner. It was remarked about these two meetings how well they were run and that the races started on time.

In January 1900 a stepping match was advertised in the Southern Star. This match was to take place on 28th January between Jack Buckley, Gortbrach, and James Leary, Cahergal, Myross, and was to be run from Kenne's, Castletownshend to Tralagogh Strand and back, for a stake of £30. The advertisements and reports never mentioned the names of the horses, which were all trotters not pacers. Stepping matches were also mentioned in the stories, which were based on real events, of Somerville and Ross, including one won by a yellow mare with "a step as fast as the tick of a watch".

Even in those early days thought and effort was being put into improving the sport and into breeding. Trotters were already being imported. In 1900 the Trotting Union of Great Britain and Ireland was compiling a Trotting Stud Book and was trying to raise the standard of racing. But earlier, in 1852, Andrew Bonar, who lived in Milltown, near Tralee, wrote a book on the breeding and rearing of horses. A chapter was devoted to trotting and he refers to a "high price for any good trotter". He also states that "the greatest performers are now brought from America where trotting is all the rage" but goes on to say that if attention were paid to breeding and training there would be nothing to prevent "us having equally as fast trotters as the Americans".

110  Rosscarbery - Past & Present

*The Gallant Man (right) winning at Bantry for the second year in a row. 1999.*

Irish Molly, foaled in 1902 at Drominidy in Drimoleague, made her first appearance in 1904 when she was ridden by her owner, Little Dan McCarthy, to see O'Donovan Rossa unveil the Maid of Erin in Skibbereen. Irish Molly, the champion of the day, won many trotting races. She also ran in, and won, flat races.

The next decade saw plenty of race meetings, again combined with sports. On Monday, 4th April 1910, three thousand people attended the races at Ballydehob. For this, and all sporting meetings of the time, train schedules were published in advance. At Ballydehob there was only one trotting match, an open race over three miles. The first prize was £4, of which the winner had to give £1 to the runner-up. The race was won by J. Burke's Maureen and second was J Mahony's Kattie. Kattie also contested the two-mile flat race, but was unplaced. Three trotting races were included in the sports day at Corran on 20th June 1917. The open was won by P. McCarthy, Drominidy, and the confined by J. Connolly.

Things did not always run smoothly and the Southern Star had plenty of correspondence complaining about judges' decisions and issuing challenges. In November 1910, referring to a trotting match at Dereeny Bridge for horses which had never won a race, Patrick Sullivan, Caheragh, claimed foul play. He stated that a member of the Committee rode his own horse part of the way against Sullivan's horse to try and get it to break, which interference failed. P. O'Driscoll, Clounkeen West, owner of the horse that was awarded the race accepted the challenge for a re-match. It should be noted that objections to judges' decisions and calls for re-runs were not confined to trotting; owners of flat horses were just as quick to air their grievances.

Reports of trotting were scarce on the ground until 1935. Both Drimoleague and Sam's Cross held races on St Stephen's Day. Only four contested the Open at Drimoleague, which was won by D.C. McCarthy's Moonshine Boy, while the Confined, in which twelve ran, went to C. Cotter's Tasty Bit. At Sam's Cross James McCarthy, Lyre, won the race for trotting cobs, while J. O'Donovan was first in the only other event, the Second Class Race.

Bantry races, held on 1st June 1936 advertised only trot and, in that, previous winners in Cork and Kerry were to be handicapped. A well-known trotter of this period was Rob Roy, owned by John Willson of Derry House, Rosscarbery.

Among the list of stallions of all sorts advertised to stand for the 1936 season, Thomas Roycroft, Lissacaha Stud, Schull, offered Aeroplane, whose sire, Aerolite, was the Champion Trotter of England. Forest Freeman seemed to be a famous trotting sire, of racers as well as driving ponies. Michael Lehane, Bantry, promoted his Bantry Boy stating that the dam, Wait and See, was an imported trotting pony which had won numerous trotting matches and was particularly commended for her stamina.

Three trotting races, along with flat races, were held at Barryroe in January 1946. C. O'Regan's Dunworley Boy won the Confined. R. Hobbs Grey Dawn the Open and J

*John Wilson of Derry House, Rosscarbery, driving his famous Rob Roy at Clonakilty Show in the early 1930's. Rob Roy died after being driven at Skibbereen Show in 1936.*

McCarthy's Barryshall Hope the other Confined. In June the same year Bantry's one trotting race, over three miles, was won by John Donovan's well-known Candy. Durrus races were always well reported in The Star and the report for 1952 mentions a bigger crowd than the previous year, which was a record one, and also that the entry was believed bigger than ever before. Familiar names were among the winners. T. McCarthy's Little Man won the Open, Flying Saucer the Consolation, James Hegarty's Split the Wind was successful in the Parish while Michael Connolly's Ocean Breeze won the Third Class Trot. Flying Saucer won the Open Trot at Ballydehob in 1953, where three trotting and three flat races were staged. Nine ran in both the Parish and the Confined, won respectively by M. Roycroft's Jockey and R. Wolfe's Charlie. Laddie from Leap had obviously not appeared yet, but did race against Flying Saucer and Little Man, among others

## PART 2

After a couple of hundred years of saddle racing of trotters only, the 1960's saw the beginning of the transformation of the sport into what it is today. In 1963 a demonstration of harness racing took place in Skibbereen, thanks to the efforts of Jerome O'Sullivan, Honorary Secretary of Skibbereen Gymkhana. Members of the Dublin Trotting Club travelled with their horses and sulkies for what was billed as "American Pony Trotting" which "must be seen to be believed". Another "spectacular attraction" at that gymkhana, which attracted over 6000 people, was Tommy Wade and his renowned half-Connemara show jumper, Dundrum. The Dublin Trotting Club made other trips to West Cork and, by the early seventies, both harness racing and pacers were firmly established.

In the mid-seventies a rift developed, with two separate organisations running race meetings. It wasn't until 1983 that the two groups, Cork County Trotting Association and the Munster Trotting and Harness Association were united, through the work and far-sightedness of James Connolly, Dunmanway. Shortly thereafter the Irish Trotting and Harness Racing Federation was formed and, in 1984, the Horseowners' Association. Also around that time, Youen Jacob imported Normandy Trotters and the relative merits of trotters vs. pacers were widely discussed. These French trotters held sway for a time, with Jolly Castle winning the 1984 All-Ireland Harness and the 1985 All-Ireland Road Championship, while Keve won the All-Ireland Harness at Skibbereen in 1985. In that same year exhibition harness races were held at both Cork and Charleville Shows.

The importation of Smokeaway

and later Hi Lo's Chief, improved the local breed of pacers. Smokeaway, out of a New Zealand mare and a U.S. sire and stood with Donal Callaghan in Schull, was responsible for five winners, and was a grandsire of a sixth, on the Tuesday of Ballabuidhe in 1988.

The arrival of the immortal Limed Hazard in 1990 opened a glorious decade for trotting. Among his achievements were three double All-Irelands in a row and eighteen unbeaten starts at Droumleena Lawn. Sounders Spirit, whose record for the mile at Central Track still stands, came to join his illustrious stable-mate, H.T. Adios, while Beauty's Forte, Blackwell Peter and Just an Angel were also imported in the early nineties. The races between these great horses created a buzz that people still talk about.

The single most significant event of the decade, however, was the opening of Central Track on the lands of Paddy and Elma Collins in 1992. At last able to race and school on a hard track West Cork horses were prepared to venture out and prove themselves. In 1993 a team of four travelled to Portmarnock and won the Inter-County there. 1999 saw Southland's Albatross become the first West Cork owned horse to win across the water, while in August of that same year Ata's Crook, trained and driven by half-owner Kieran Sheehy, won the prestigious Roosevelt Cup at Tir Prince in Wales, setting a course record for trotters while he was at it.

The unification of the three governing trotting bodies in the whole of Ireland also took place in 1999. Now called the Irish Harness Racing Club the chairmanship is on a rotational basis. The 2001 Chairman is Kevin McLoughlin of the Northern Ireland Standardbred Association.

With the wealth of stallions currently in West Cork the series of Sire Stakes, administered by Jim McCarthy and Gerard Carey, have proved very successful. Trotting has kept up with the times and the vibrant ITHRF website, www.ithrf.8m.com attracts hits from all over the world,

All those owners, jockeys and fans who kept trotting alive over the years might be surprised at the changes in the sport. Amy O'Reilly's win, when representing Ireland in the Celtic Invitational Ladies Challenge in August 2001, and Bright Sun and Derry McCarthy lowering the colours of Dublin's best in a free for all in September, both at Portmarnock, are just two recent achievements which show how far trotting has come.

## *ACKNOWLEDGEMENTS:*

Thanks to the Southern Star, and particularly Anne Kelleher, for assistance and to Geraldine McCarthy for her help on the introduction of harness racing to West Cork.

# Rathbarry and Castlefreke

by Michael Collins

The Barrys were among the principal Anglo-Norman families to gain control of large areas of Cork, shortly after 1180, and were in the Galley Head/Rathbarry area until Arthur Freke leased it from them in 1618.

The first of the Barrys to settle in Cork was Philip Barry who was granted lands in East Cork in 1180. Later the Barrys came into possession of lands in different parts of the county:
The Barry Mor at Barry's Court
The Barry MacAdam in Rathcormac
The Barry Og at Kinsale- Innishannon
And The Barry Rua of Ibane and Barryroe

The Barrys came into possession of the lands in Ibane and Barryroe when they succeeded the Butlers, either through marriage or otherwise. Nicholas Bui Barry built Timoleague Castle in 1213. They built Dundeady Castle, near Galley Head, in 1215. In 1427, Randal Og Barry built Rathbarry Castle, or to be more correct, re-built or re-constructed it. It seems that there was an old Fort or castle on this site that went back beyond the coming of the Normans. Fr. Coombes tells us that an earlier name for this area was Rath an Oileain (the land around the rath was practically an island). Another interesting fact was the discovery of a hoard of Viking coins at Rathbarry. They were Anglo-Saxon coins and dated from 945 AD. We know that the Vikings were in this district (i.e. Rosscarbery) in the latter part of the tenth century. Whatever the story of the Vikings at Rathbarry we will never know, but the finding of these coins suggest that there was some kind of structure there before the year 1000AD, perhaps an old fort or a Christian settlement.

In the thirteenth century the Irish began to fight back against the Normans with some success. At the Battle of Callan, near Kenmare, in 1261, the Irish led by the McCarthys defeated the Normans. The Barrys and the other Norman families were pushed back towards the sea. Fineen McCarthy took Dundeady Castle and burnt Dunoure Castle. At a battle or skirmish near Ringrone Castle, Fineen was killed. The loss of this great Irish leader allowed the Normans to hold on to

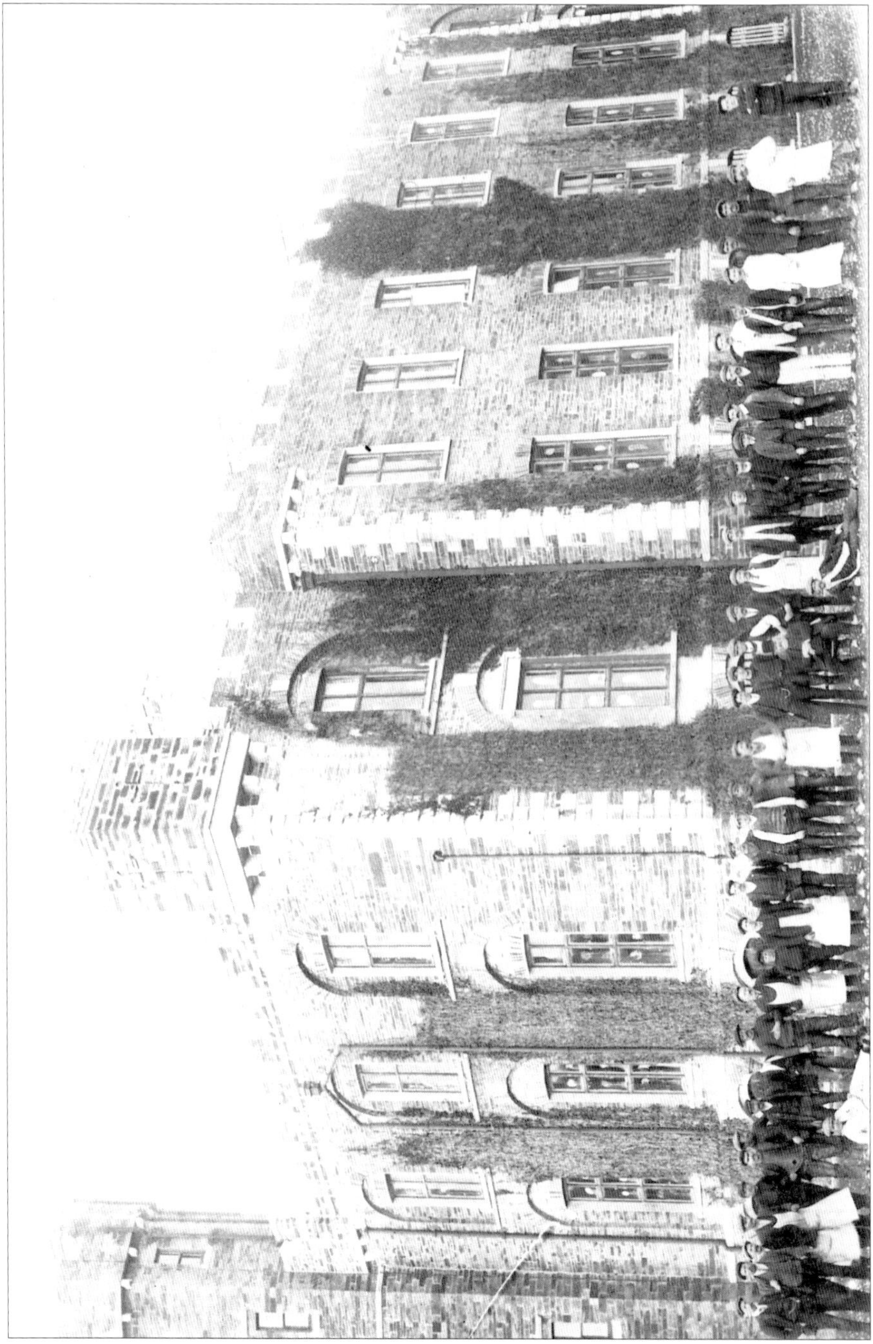

the peninsulas along the Cork coast. As time evolved they held Ibane and Barryroe, Barry Og held Kinsale –Innishannon area, the Barry Mor were around Cork harbour and the De Courceys held the Old Head of Kinsale.

William Maol Barry or William Fitzdavid Barry was in control of Ibane and Rathbarry in 1331. He was the brother of David Fitzdavid, Lord Barrymore. William Maol built Timoleague Friary in 1373 and was buried there with his wife Margaret de Courcey in 1375. Their descendants formed the separate lineage of the Barrys of Ibane and Barryroe and their son Laurence was the first to be called Ruadha or Red, hence the first Barryroe.

There was peace and prosperity in Ibane and Barryroe from then until 1550. The prosperity came through the influence of the Franciscan Friary in Timoleague and the Cistercian monastery in Abbeymahon. The monks cultivated and farmed the land very effectively, and industrious farmers learned from them. The Barrys were also great seafarers with such families as the Cowhigs, O'Heas, Fahys, O'Flynns and others. They seemed to do a lot of trading with the continent. In 1507, James Fitzdavid Barry was lost at sea, with others, on return from a pilgrimage to St. James of Compostello. There were also mentions of pilgrimages in 1472, 1482 and 1518.

Problems arose for the Barrys after this time. James Fitzrichard's grandfather, who was also James, married a McCarthy woman from Muskerry but this marriage was found to be illegal, so he put her aside and married a McCarthy Riach woman, to whom he had previously been betrothed. This caused fighting between the Barrys of Ibane. James Fitzrichard Barry of Rathbarry was fighting the family of David Down Barry of Timoleague who was his first cousin. Two of David's sons were slain and two more fled to the Earl of Desmond for protection. James Fitzrichard seemed to succeed.

Another problem arose as Lord Barrymore had no male heir, his daughter married Lord Power of Waterford, but this was not acceptable to the Barrys. Consequently James Fitzrichard of Rathbarry was elected Lord Barrymore in 1557 and Viscount Buttevant and a member of the Irish Parliament in 1559.

In 1559, at the time of the suppression of the monasteries, he applied for a lease of Timoleague Friary, which was granted. He allowed the monks to stay on, where they remained until the time of Cromwell. At this stage, we are on the eve of the Desmond rebellion. James joined on the side of the Desmonds, his cousins, and was captured and imprisoned in Dublin Castle where he died on April 10th 1581.

His son David succeeded him in the wars and was defeated by the English commander Captain Zouch and later submitted to the King of England. He was pardoned on 24th August 1582. He received back his land and title for the payment of a fine of £600. David Fitzjames became Lord Barrymore and his brother, William, got Ibane and Barryroe. William died in 1584 and his lands, including Rathbarry, were returned to David, Lord Barrymore. William's wife and son were allowed to stay on in Lisleagh Castle with some land and an allowance. Rathbarry remained with Lord Barrymore and around this time he rented it to a Mr. Walsh. It was from his grandson (also Lord Barrymore) that Arthur Freke leased Rathbarry Castle in 1618.The siege of Rathbarry in 1641, which lasted 239 days took place during the run of this lease.

The wind of change started to blow on Rathbarry, as on all of Ireland. Munster had just been ravaged in the Desmond wars, and now the Nine Years War was upon us. Ibane and Rathbarry did not escape - it was raided by both sides. O'Neal came in 1599 and because Lord Barrymore opposed him, he raided his land in Ibane and Barryroe. The English treated Ibane and Rathbarry likewise, when they raided West Cork.

1601 brought the Spaniards and the Battle of Kinsale. The Spaniards probably visited Rathbarry and there is some mention of Red Hugh O' Donnell passing through here after Kinsale. Be that as it may, Captain Harvey took over Rathbarry Castle for Her Majesty, Queen Elizabeth 1, on May 1st 1602. Of course, Rathbarry was still the property of Lord Barrymore, David Fitzjames Barry, who was a staunch Catholic to the end. He died in 1617. His son David pre-deceased him, so his title passed to his grandson, also David but he was still a minor (twelve years old). David being a juvenile, the title came under the control of Richard Boyle, Lord Cork. Boyle had David married to his own daughter Alice in 1621 when they were both sixteen years of age. David, who became a Protestant, was made Earl of Barrymore 1628. From this time the Barrymore title became pro-English and remained so until the title ran out in 1828.

Back in Rathbarry, after the Battle of Kinsale in 1601, the morale of the people was low and things were slipping more and more into English control. The people's lands and religions were slipping away from them. Rathbarry was now under the influence of Lord Cork and was leased to Arthur Freke in 1618 for sixty-three years.

The next mention we have of Rathbarry is 23 years later, during the 1641 rebellion. When this rebellion erupted, having started in the north on the 23rd October, it quickly spread southwards. Glandore is said to have seen the first of the action in the south. The Gaelic people came out against the Planters and the various agents of British rule, forcing these people to take refuge and shelter in the garrison towns and local castles. In Rathbarry Castle, Arthur Freke found he was crowded with Planters and Protestants taking shelter. On 14th February, the Irish threw up a siege around Rathbarry Castle that lasted until 9th October. This turned out to be the longest siege in Irish History.

The local Irish leaders were John Og Barry and Tadgh Barry of Dundeady, Tadgh O' Hea of Kilgarriff, Florence McCarthy of Benduff and many others. The rebels were rampant. There appears to have been a great show of strength at first. The Irish approached Freke, hoping for a compromise whereby he would hand over the castle to them for the safety of himself and his household. But Freke was not having any of it. As the siege progressed, there were almost nightly raids on his livestock, cattle, sheep and horses.

By April, or around the time of planting crops, things seemed to get a bit quieter as many of the Irish moved back to their farms. By this stage Freke seemed to be putting most of his stock inside the walls of the castle every night. Freke tells us in his own account of the siege that on Trinity Sunday, 22nd May, Philip O' Sullivan camped with 200 men, and in a cleverly planned move, chased away almost all of Freke's animals after he had let them out to graze in the early morning. Arthur Freke admits he was in dire straits with all his animals gone, no salt to cure food, and more and more people coming into the castle. There were now over 200 people to feed and he had received no communications from his friends in Kinsale or Bandon. They tried raiding into enemy territory for cattle, but failed when some of his party were killed. They then built a boat on Lough Rath Bharraig and managed to reach Castlehaven for help. A Captain Browne sailed to Rathbarry and managed to come in quite close. He picked up ninety-two people and took them to Kinsale. On Sunday 17th July, Freke says he was running low in ammunition, men and provisions. So, when he saw a large army approaching the Castle, Freke thought it was McCarthy's army intent on a final assault. But no, they were English. Lord Forbes, a free-lance mercenary, had arrived in Kinsale and had marched to Bandon, raiding Timoleague and Clonakilty on his way, before leaving half of his men in Clonakilty. He brought with him thirty-two cows and bulls, which he probably 'picked up' on his way from Clonakilty. Forbes had not finished his meal in the castle when a message reached him that his men were under attack in Clonakilty. He hastened back to Clonakilty, taking some of Freke's fighting men and leaving some of his own, who were tired and sickly.

When Forbes arrived in Clonakilty, he fought the attackers and chased them towards Inchydoney, where 600 died, either by the sword or by drowning, as the tide was in. Forbes did not return to Rathbarry, as the story there was just as bad as before – a raiding party had taken most of the cows and bulls (probably the original owner). After these incidents, the siege became tough and no quarter was given. One wonders why the Irish did not push a final assault. Freke was vulnerable and he really feared McCarthy's army. As for John Og Barry (Dundeady), he adopted a much softer stance and seemed to think that time was on his side. His hope was to take Freke out as quietly as possible and he was also eager to take possession of the Castle. On the 9th August, during a fierce gale, Sir Samuel Cooke's ship managed to land for a very short time, leaving some provisions and ammunition, and taking a few people on board for Kinsale. As he was passing Dundeady, he fired a few volleys of cannon at Dundeady Castle.

John Og Barry seems to have panicked, because a few days later eighteen English men whom Barry held as prisoners were released and made their way to the castle. To add to Freke's plight some Irish prisoners held at Rathbarry escaped.

*Building workers at Castlefreke, c. 1912.*

Towards the end of August, John Og Barry stepped up the pressure. With 400 men, he made an assault on Rathbarry Castle, but the defenders had walled up the gateways and other entrances. Barrys men entrenched at various points outside the walls, but Freke's men built his ramparts higher, so that they could fire down onto the trenches. A point that must not be forgotten is the strength of this little fortress. It was almost impregnable. On St. Michaelmas Day, 29th September, Barry made another assault on the castle with colours and placards flying.

As a last resort, two men were sent out of the castle by night and made their way to Bandon. A few days later Freke was astonished to see Barry's men move quietly away. On the following day, 9th October, relief arrived from Bandon. Two hundred and thirty nine days after the siege had started, the castle was relieved by Charles Vavasor and Jepson. A garrison of about eighty people was taken to Bandon and Arthur Freke and his family, along with Lieutenant Beecher, left Rathbarry Castle in flames, having started the fire themselves.

Following the siege, the Irish took over Rathbarry. The Barrys held sway for only a short time, as the English (Bandonians) returned a year later and took Clonakilty, Rosscarbery and Rathbarry. With Arthur Freke once more in possession of his castle and lands, this would mark the end of the Barrys in Rathbarry, and see the continuation of the Frekes for over 300 years (1618-1921).

Near the end of the siege, or just after it, Arthur Freke's son Percy was born. In 1671, he married his second cousin, Elizabeth Freke, a grand-daughter of Thomas Freke, whose brother, William, came to Ireland as a Planter in the 1580's or 1590's. His son Arthur was born around 1603. In 1675, Elizabeth and Percy had a son, whom they named Ralph. As Elizabeth would have preferred to live in England (Percy preferred to live here), they spent a lot of time travelling to and fro. The sixty-three year lease of Rathbarry Castle expired in 1681and Percy bought out Rathbarry Castle from Lord Barrymore for £1400. In 1684, Percy Freke leased Rathbarry Castle to John Hull for forty-one years at £250 per annum. Hull had been a steward for Freke but no sooner had the ink dried on their written agreement, than they were in bitter dispute. The Freke family went back to England, much to Elizabeth's delight, and they settled down happily there, until 1688 when the war broke out between William of Orange and King James. Percy got itchy feet again and was soon back in Ireland where he fought in the battle of the Boyne as a Colonel in the Bandon regiment. In the meantime John Hull had died and during the Jacobite war, Owen McCarthy held Rathbarry Castle for

King James.

In November 1692, England having won the war and the Irish having withdrawn, the Frekes returned to Rathbarry, only to find it burnt down. We are told that there were only two rooms fit to live in. Nevertheless, Percy seemed to flourish during the 1690's, being made County Sheriff in 1694 and also an MP.

In 1699, Ralph, Percy's son, married Elizabeth Mead, daughter of Sir John Mead of Ballintubber and consequently came into land in Queen's county. Percy returned to England and died on 2nd May 1707. In 1713, through his mother's influence, Ralph Freke was made a Baronet (Sir), the first in the Freke family. His mother now lived in England where she died in April 1718. Ralph and Elizabeth had three sons and one daughter; Percy jnr, John, Ralph jnr and Grace. Sir Ralph Freke died in 1718; aged forty-three and his wife married James, the 4th Baron Kingston. Sir Percy jnr became the 2nd Baronet and an MP for Baltimore. He had two sons, Ralph (who pre-deceased him in 1727) and John Redmond, and one daughter Grace who married John Evans of Bulgaden Hall. Sir Percy died in 1728 and was succeeded by John Redmond, 3rd Baronet, who died in 1758. His sister Grace's second son, John Evans, succeeded to the title and land to become 4th Baronet.

The families of the Carberys contain the history of both the Evans and the Frekes. The Frekes and Evans came to Ireland, after the Desmond rebellion in the reign of Queen Elizabeth. John Evans settled in the Limerick district, where they were merchants and financiers and traded in forfeited lands. Over a period of time, they acquired money and possessions, after the 1641 rebellion and again after the Treaty of Limerick. George Evans, Barrister of Law, and grandson of the 1st John Evans acquired Bulgaden Hall from the Fox family, as well as other lands in the Limerick and Cork areas. George married Mary Eyre, of Eyrecourt, Galway. They had a son George who, in 1703, married Anne, daughter of William Stafford of Northampton, and this George became the 1st Lord Carbery under in 1715. It was through the union of these two families in the marriage of Grace Freke and John Evans that the title of Lord Carbery comes to Castlefreke.

Sir John Redmond Freke died in 1758 and his lands and Castle in Rathbarry passed to his nephew John Evans, who adopted the name Evans-Freke, and became the 4th Baronet, Sir John Evans-Freke.

A census of Rathbarry parish, compiled in 1765 by Rev. Horatio Townsend, Vicar of Rathbarry, makes no mention of the Evans or the Frekes being in Rathbarry at this time. Rathbarry must have been in a poor state as it was burnt down three times in the 17th century.

We have seen the standing of the Freke family at low ebb but all that changed after the death of the 4th Baronet in 1768 and the arrival of another Sir John Evans-Freke the 5th Baronet.

In 1780, he decided to build a new residence in the town land of Gortagreanane, a short distance away, overlooking the old Rathbarry Castle. The new residence was a rectangular building and enjoyed magnificent views of the strands and Rosscarbery Bay. It was later changed to a more castle-like shape when Lord Carbery commissioned Sir Richard Morrison in 1820, a pupil of Gandon and designer of the Pro-Cathedral in Dublin. Sir John Evans-Freke inherited the title of Lord Carbery from his second cousin, the 5th Lord Carbery John Evans of Bulgaden Hall, Limerick, in 1807, to become the 6th Lord Carbery and the first to live in Castlefreke. In 1825, he had a new Church built on the estate. A Rectory was already built in 1800 and he was responsible for building some of the lodges, houses, avenues and for the whole plan and shape of the estate.

In the vote in the Irish Parliament, he voted against the Act of Union with Westminster, even though he would gain £15000 for his seat as M.P. He died in 1845 and was succeeded by his nephew Lord George Patrick, 7th Baron, who died in 1889. His brother William Charles Evans-Freke became the 8th Baron and died in 1894 and his son Algernon William George, 9th Baron, succeeded him in May 1895.

Algie, as he was affectionately called, married Mary Toulmin and they had two sons, John in 1892 and Ralph in 1897. Lord Algernon the 9th Baron, died at the very young age of 30 years in 1898 and there was a granite high cross erected over his grave on the hill of Croghna, overlooking the Long Strand. John the 10th Baron was only six years old when his father died. He came of age in 1913 and succeeded to the title. He is said to have flown the tricolour at Castlefreke castle. The castle was badly damaged by fire and was re-built using insurance monies between 1910 and 1913.

This young Lord Carbery is said to be the first Irishman to own an aeroplane. He gave exhibitions of flying at Clonakilty Show and at other venues throughout West Cork. He served in the Air force during the 1914-1918 war. Lord Carbery was a member of The House of Lords and a member of many other societies, such as the Board of Baltimore Fisheries School.

Shortly after the war, he renounced his title, decided to sell the property at Castlefreke and emigrate to Kenya. The sale of the castle was entrusted to a local firm of solicitors. Having changed hands a few times, it was eventually held by a syndicate led by Ms Fitzmaurice. They sold it to the Land Commission in the 1930's and after the outbreak of World War II, the Land Commission divided the land among the local farmers.

During World War II, or the Emergency period as it was known, the Castle was occupied by the Army, the 38th-39th Battalions. After the war, the Upton boys (The Boys of Upton Industrial School) spent their summer holidays there.

In 1952, a local man purchased the castle, but due to the excessive high rates, it was dismantled and the roof, floors, windows, doors etc sold off. This was a sad ending to a once stately house, with it's magnificent hall spiral staircases and dining room, as well as the adjoining garden and woodlands.

*Presentation of jerseys to Mount St. Michael School, left to right, Stephen Hicks, Michael Keohane, Colman Milner making presenation, Bart Kerrisk, principal*

# Glandore Classic Boat Regatta

*by Don Healey*

For the fifth time, the West Cork harbour of Glandore hosted the popular Classic Regatta and Summer School. The Summer School included many interesting talks, including Donal Lynch's History of the Six-Oar Gig.

Some yachts stopped off in Glandore on their transatlantic voyage to take part in the Regatta as a warm up for the America's Cup Jubilee, which was held in Cowes on the Isle of Wight in August 2001. The J-class yacht Velsheda was expected but had to divert to Scotland with engine problems. The 95' long Sincerity and the 65' Fife Solway Maid entered, as well as many of our loyal following of West Cork yachts and traditional boats, including the fleet of Heir Island Sloops. These are wonderful day sailing sloops designed and built close to Baltimore by Gubby Williams.

On Wednesday 18th the Glandore Bay Race was held, between Galley Head and Toe Head, in winds of force 6-7 which made for exciting racing. Several boats were forced to retire due to damage. On Thursday there was a race to the Fastnet Rock for the larger yachts and to the Kowloon Bridge mark at the Stag Rocks for the smaller boats. Conditions were a total contrast with the previous day with force 1-2 winds and calm seas.

The Minister for Agriculture, Food and Rural Development, Joe Walsh TD, officially opened the Classic Boat Regatta on Friday evening. A local crew of junior buccaneers and pirates led by Don Healy raised the tricolour to formally launch the weekend's events. On Saturday there was more racing, but a private race developed between the two Bristol Channel Pilot Cutters, Annabelle J and Marguerite. Annabelle J was built in 1996 using the original plans of Marguerite, built in 1892. The two boats were very evenly matched and it was more or less a draw.

The highlight of the week was the Parade of Sail, when all yachts sailed past and saluted the Flag; this made a most spectacular sight for those ashore. It was also quite exciting for those participating and required a high degree of skill, co-ordination and sobriety!! The parade of Sail was completed by the Dutch sail-training vessel, a three-masted

*Don Healy (left) in pirate costume leads the parade for the opening of the Classic Boat Regatta.*

topsail schooner, Oosterschelde.

The week finished with a spectacular firework display over Glandore Harbour on Sunday night. The next Classic Boat Regatta and Summer School is scheduled for July 2003.
Parade of Sail Prizewinners - Glandore Classic Regatta 2001
Best Turned out Classic Yacht: Blue Leopard
Best Turned out Work Boat: Macalla, a West Cork mackerel boat
Best Turned out Dayboat: Cobblers a Cornish Cobble
Best Turned out Dragon: Pan, Jan Panman
Best Turned out Cruising Yacht: CiMor from Wales
Best Salute: Spirit of Oysterhaven
Best Local Traditional Boat: Fionn Long Island Lobster Boat
The Oldest Boat, Bristol Channel Pilot Cutter: Marguerite, 1889
The Olympic Prize: Bill Masser Wagtail
Most unusual name SAVVEDRA: Bill Neate
Most Sporting Crew: Jaynor D Brown
The boat that came farthest: Sincerity, from Antigua
Best Female Skipper: Frances Lynch Phoenix and Seal Song
Best Dressed Crew: George Radley and Crew on Querida
Most venerable Crew: Murre Mr. Stanley Woods.
Youngest Crew: Mini, the Mckenna Family, Union Hall.
Best Supporting Yacht: Penultimate, George Lipscombe.
Sir Lancelot trophy (for coming to the rescue): George Radley.
Most Mutinous Captain: Capt. Guy Perrin of MAB.
Wrong side of Adam Island Award: Milverton, Dermot O'Sullivan

Boat of the Regatta JLS design Trophy went to:
Roger Sandiford's classic Fife Solway Maid
This trophy, donated by the Kinsale based Yacht Design Team, is a very impressive and unusual 3D chart of Glandore Harbour.

Concours D'elegance: Norwegian Fife Sincerity

Overall winners by Class for Glandore Classic Regatta 2001
Dayboats: Theresa Gubby Williams
Work Boats: Eileen Rruin replica Falmouth Work boat. Delapp family
DRAGONS: Fafner Donald Street III
Class II: Querida Cork harbour One design George Radley
Class I: Brynoth, H Sherrard

*Autumn History School Committee: left to right, Denise Sparks, Jerry Wycherley, Fachtna O'Callaghan, Kate Wycherley, Mary Buckley, Michael Harte, Cal Hyland, Paddy O'Donovan, Con O'Callaghan and Michael Tobin.*

# First Autumn History School a huge success

*by Michael Tobin*

The first Autumn History School in Rosscarbery was held from 28th to 30th September 2001. It was based on the life, works and legacy of the socialist and philosopher William Thompson 1775-1833. Thompson, who lived in Clounkeen East, near Rosscarbery, influenced Horace Plunkett, who pioneered the co-operative movement.

The first speaker on Friday 28th was Dr. Dolores Dooley, from the Department of Philosophy, U.C.C. Dr. Dooley has undertaken major research on Thompson, which has been published by the Cork University Press.

Mr. John Tyrell, Director General of ICOS (Irish Co-operative Organisation Society), spoke on the Irish Co-operative Movement. Mr. Tyrell has played an active role in the development of the Irish position on the Common Agricultural Policy.

Mr. Donncha O'Dulaing was the guest speaker at the official dinner that evening.

Mr Padraic White, former Managing Director of the Industrial Development Authority, was the chairperson for the talks on Saturday. He commented that three of the speakers were from Belfast and spoke of the relevance of co-operation and equality as issues in the Irish community.

Vincent Geoghegan, Professor of political theory at Queen's University, Belfast, spoke on Henry McCormack who Thompson appointed as one of the trustees of his Will. McCormack was much influenced by Thompson's ideas. Prof. Geoghegan said that Thompson and McCormack were part of the first wave of socialism in Ireland.

Mr. John Lougheed works in the EU-funded Rural Development programmes in the English speaking member states. He made a comparison between LEADER (Continental, National and Local funding for community development) and the principles laid down in Thompson's Practical Directions.

Prof. Alun Evans, of Queen's University, Belfast, spoke on the medical aspects of Practical Directions.

A monument to Thompson, which had been erected by the Historical Society, built by Michael Harte and

Speakers at the Autumn History School, from left, John Lougheed, Dolores Dooley, Cal Hyland, Michael Tobin, Alan Evans, Tom Duddy, Padraig White, Vincent Geoghegan and Liam O'Regan.

Charlie McCarthy was officially unveiled by Mr. Joe Walsh, T.D., Minister for Agriculture and Food and Rural Development, on Saturday afternoon. This was followed by a tour of locations associated with Thompson and his commune.

Liam O'Regan, Editor and proprietor of the Southern Star, was chairperson on Sunday. He commended the Historical Society for their journals and work.

Cal Hyland, antiquarian bookseller and local historian, spoke about Fr. Jeremiah O'Callaghan, a socially conscious local curate, who opposed usury. Like Thompson, Fr. O'Callaghan was very sympathetic to the poor.

Dr. Tom Duddy, of UCG, spoke on Producing Happiness. Thompson believed that "Kindly feelings and benevolent conduct would expand in co-operative societies. Virtue would consist in blessing and being blessed". Love of wealth and power scarcely exist in co-operative communities. Dr. Duddy was the final speaker in a very stimulating and successful Autumn School.

# DIARY
# October 2000 – September 2001

### OCTOBER 2000

| | |
|---|---|
| 5 | AGM of Rosscarbery & District Historical Society |
| 8 | Walk to Castlefreke |
| 11 | Johnny O'Mahony, Bohonagh, died. R.I.P |
| 14 | Reunion of Leaving Cert Class of 1970 |
| 15 | Carbery Rangers lost by 2 points to Ilen Rovers in The West Cork Junior Football Final |
| 19 | Donncha O Dualaing addressed the Historical Society |
| 29 | Lisavaird Root and Grain Show |

### NOVEMBER

| | |
|---|---|
| 8 | Hanora Brosnan, Barleyhill, died. R.I.P. |
| 9 | Michael O'Mahony, Leap, died.R.I.P. |
| 15 | 103FM celebrated 10 years on air |
| 16 | Denis Calnan, Glandore, died. R.I.P. |
| 19 | Walk to Myross |
| 22 | Johnny O'Driscoll, Gortroe, died. R.I.P. |
| 24 | Paddy Lane, Newtown, died. R.I.P |
| 29 | Nellie O' Donovan, Clonakilty & |

*A1*
*Michael Daly, Annette Donoghue, Neil Dugnan, Rosemary Daly-taking part in the Carrigfada Walk.*
*A2*
*Trotting Races on The Causeway*

*Rosscarbery Diary*

Reenascreena, died. R.I.P.
30   Brigid Lawlor, Rosscarbery, died R.I.P.
Kate Ann Hill, Leap, died. R.I.P.

## DECEMBER

2   Margaret Hayes, Bohonagh, died. R.I.P.
4   Dolores Froehner-Fleury, Rosscarbery, died. R.I.P.
Bella Shorten, Courleigh North, died. R.I.P.
7   Volume Two of Rosscarbery Past & Present launched by Donncha O Dualaing in the Pilgrims Rest
10   Ross Under 16 footballers defeated Ballinhassig in their County semi-final
17   Annual walk to Drombeg Stone Circle cancelled because of heavy rain. There was a brilliant Sunset
20   Ross Primary Schools' Carol Singing for patients atClonakilty Hospital
26   Carrigfada Walk took place despite heavy snowfalls.
31   Mary Josephine (Jo) O'Donovan, Rosscarbery, died. R.I.P.

2001

## JANUARY

14   Trotting Races on the Causeway were

*A2*
*Fachtna O'Callaghan,*
*Paddy O'Donovan,*
*Con O'Callaghan,*
*Dean Chris Peters,*
*Mary Hoseason,*
*Donncha O Dualaing,*
*Michael Harte.*

*A3*
*Rosscarbery Past & Present launched by Donncha O Dualaing.*

*B1*
*Michael O'Sullivan, Finbarr O'Keeffe (retirement presentation), Carmel O'Keeffe and Nora Hubbert.*

*B2*
*O'Connell family appear on RTE's Family Matters.*

revived after a number of years and, hopefully, will now be repeated annually.

Brilliant sunshine, an unmatchable course, thorough preparation, a record entry, generous sponsorship, good stewarding and many other positive factors contributed to the outstanding success of the day and provided entertainment for the 3000 specators.

18  Desmond Hill spoke on The Economic War at the monthly Meeting of the Rosscarbery & District Historical Society
19  Finbarr O'Keefe, Rosscarbery, died. R.I.P. James O'Keeffe, Gurrane, died. R.I.P.
20  Ross Minor Footballers were defeated by Erin's Own in the County Final at Ballygarvan 0-5 to 1-6
22  New Downeen Water Scheme started
24  Mount St Michael defeated Crosshaven 55-53 in Cork Colleges Basketball Final
25  AGM of Girls Football. The following were appointed – Chair Liz Hayes, Deputy Margaret Hayes, Secretary Pat Lane, Assistant Geraldine Hayes, Treasurers Ann Hayes and Liz Hayes
28  Walk from Long Strand to Galley Head included a guided tour of The lighthouse

*Rosscarbery Diary*

## FEBRUARY

2   Scor Na Bpáistí County Final in Inniscarra Hall
3   Presentation to Denis Hayes on his retirement from Lisavaird Co-op
5   Daniel O'Brien, Rosscarbery, died. R.I.P.
12  Margaret Cullinane, Cahirbeg, died. R.I.P.
    First AGM of Rosscarbery Women's Group
15  Rickard Deasy spoke about The Deasys of West Cork and Clonakilty to almost 100 people at the Historical Society meeting. Many of those attending were members of Cumann Seanchais Clanna Coillte and had travelled from far and near. Mr Deasy was accompanied by his mother, in her late seventies but a great example of youthful enthusiasm, and by his nephew Damien Deasy. Richard's talk took us back to the 16th century and family diaries kept in the 17th and 18th centuries gave a comprehensive and engrossing view of the family's history and lore.
17  Presentation of Medals to Under-age footballers
18  Presentation of Medals to U-12 Girls Football Team during a Disco in the Celtic Ross Hotel

*B3*
*Mount St. Michael Meitheal team, front l to r, Kevin O'Connor, Peter O'Donovan, Stephen Hicks, Michael Keohane, Mary Calnan, Eoin O'Shea, Back row, Mairead Cadogan, Marcella O'Sullivan, Eimear Leonard, Margaret Dillon, Louise Canty, Brian Hayes.*

*B4*
*Eoghan Harris (back) with Michelle Mitton, Joan Hyland, Grainne Hyland, Jonathan Mitton, Dean Chris Peters and Sarah Hodson.*

|    |    |
|---|---|
| 20 | All-Ireland Colleges Basketball Finals were held at Mount St Michael<br>Kitt Hodnett, Downeen, died. R.I.P. Gathering of past pupils, parents and friends at the Convent. Fr. Bertie O'Mahony celebrated Mass |
| 25 | Seven Heads Walk — After this date all walks, meetings, football matches, pitch & putt, trotting, marts and markets etc etc were postponed indefinitely because of the threat of foot and mouth disease. The people united in a splendid show of solidarity with the farmers. |
| 25 | At the AGM of Carbery Rangers all outgoing officers were re-elected |

### MARCH

|    |    |
|---|---|
| 2  | Women's World Day of Prayer celebrated in Ross Convent |
| 6  | First adult class in European Computer Driving Licence at Mount St Michael |
| 10 | William Hayes, Newtown, died. R.I.P. |
| 12 | Joan Smith, The Warren, died. R.I.P. |
| 16 | Frances Griffin, Burgatia, died. R.I.P. |
| 21 | Confirmation Day in Ross |
| 23 | Jim and Margaret O'Connell and family, Owenahincha, appeared on Family Matters on RTE 2 television Photo |

*C1*
*John Hayes, Batt Duggan, David Lombard and Gearoid Ryan won All-Ireland U-16 Rugby medals*

*C2*
*Emma and Jerh Fitzpatrick with bowling trophies.*

Rosscarbery Diary

| 25 | Fachtna O'Sullivan, Tullyneaskey, died. R.I.P. |
| 27 | Paddy Hayes, Castlefreke, died. R.I.P. |
| 29 | Michael Crowley, Coolcraheen, died. R.I.P. At the AGM of the Pitch & Putt Club Jackie Kingston was elected President and Pat Mannion, Chairman and Captain |

### APRIL

| 2 | Fashion Show at Celtic Ross Hotel presented by students of the Transition Year, Mount St Michael and the Profile Model Agency |
| 5 | Jasper Wolfe, Downeen, died. R.I.P. |
| 7 | Doheny's defeated Carbery Rangers in U-21 Football First Round Poker Classic in Ross Lodge & Tavern in aid of renovations in the Parish Church |
| 13, 14, 15 | Rosscarbery Oyster Festival was a huge success. Beautiful weather was a big help as was the fact that there were no competing attractions in the locality. Good organisation and advertising contributed a lot. There was entertainment to suit all tastes. The main events were; the Festival Dinner Dance |

*C3*

*Switch played at a fund-raiser for the Friends of Children of Chernobyl in the Pike Bar. Front l. to r., Dick Kingston, Ann Kelly, Pascal O'Brien, Brendan Collins. Back, Mary Rose O'Brien, Catherine Kingston, Sonny O'Leary, three members of Switch group, and Lorraine Collins.*

*C4*

*Eoin Milner, Peter Hourihane, Andrew McCarthy and Peter O'Donovan, cycled to Killarney and back to raise funds for Cancer Treatment*

D1
*European Computer Driving Licence Graduation in Darrara.*
*Front, l to r., Ann Nugent, Tim Looney, Joe Walsh, T.D., J.J. Harty, Angela Murphy, Eugene Hayes. Back row, James Hurley, Noel Tobin, Miriam Daly, Eileen Dempsey, Joan O'Donovan, Rose McNulty, Mary Calnan, Mary Shanahan, Fionnuala Galwey, Geraldine O'Mahony and Joanne Prouse.*

D2
*Belarus bound students, Matthew Tuohy Elaine Flavin and Kevin Tuohy with Bart Kerrisk, principal.*

and Sunday's Tea Dance, both held in the Celtic Ross Hotel. There was Beat on the Street, discos in the Courthouse Bar Marquee, Pitch and Putt, football and even a bouncy castle.

## MAY

1 Mount St Michael's Junior Footballers reached the Cork Colleges County Final
2 John Santry, Tulligee, died. R.I.P.
   Michael Collins, Reenascreena, died. R.I.P.
3 Ellen Hayes, Ardagh, died. R.I.P.
11 Art and Literature Festival was opened by Eoghan Harris
11,12, 13 Art and Literature Festival The highlight of this year's festival, from the literary angle, was Gearoid McEoin's talk on Saltair na Rann.

This epic is supposed to have been written in the Rosscarbery monastery around 988AD. The author was most likely Airbeirteach Mac Cosse, Principal of the College of Ross at about that time.

A very significant figure in our history Airbeirteach is believed to have been taken hostage by the Danes to Scattery

Island in the Shannon estuary. His significance may be gauged from the report that Brian Boru paid the ransom demanded for him and had him returned to his post in Rosscarbery.

Airbeirteach's epic poem/story, Saltair na Rann runs to 8000 lines and is the longest poem ever written in the course of our history. It ranges from the story of creation to the history and geography of the world, the Old Testament at length, the New Testament briefly and several other topics treated in poetic style, and with poetic licence.

Gearoid's talk was a revelation in terms of history and literature. Saltair na Rann adds another huge dimension to Ross' many claims to fame: St Fachtna, with his monastery, college and Teampaillin, the Benedictine Priory (Ross Abbey), the Cathedral, etc. etc.

Several galleries around the town, from the Social Centre to the Convent, displayed the highest quality works of crafts, paintings, prints, pottery, photography, antique and modern lace and quilting. A splendid exhibition and an achievement to be very proud of indeed.

13   Ross Pilgrimage to Knock

*D3*
*Millennium Mass At*
*Teampallain Fachtna*

*D4*
*Karen Dalton on*
*Woodfield Pride*

| | |
|---|---|
| 19 | First Communion in Parish Church Homing Pigeons were released from Ross destined for points in Leinster & Ulster |
| 20 | Four Ross boys – John Hayes, Batt Duggan, Gearoid Ryan and David Lombard won All-Ireland U-16 Rugby medals with Clonakilty Rugby Club |
| 26 | Vincent Daly, Ardagh, died. R.I.P. |
| 27 | Women's Group held a Cake & Plant Sale. Proceeds were shared between Friends of Children of Chernobyl and Marymount Hospice |
| 28 | John Connolly, Bandon, died. R.I.P |

## JUNE

| | |
|---|---|
| 7 | A Black Kite was seen in Castlefreke Wood, a rare visitor. |
| 8 | Catherine Kelly, Rosscarbery, died. R.I.P. |
| 10 | Clean up of Long Strand organised by Rathbarry Tidy Towns Committee |
| 11, 12, 13 | Peter O'Donovan, Peter Hourihane, Eoin Milner, Andrew McCarthy cycled to Killarney and back to raise funds for Cancer Treatment |
| 15 | Jerome Nagle, Gahanive, died. R.I.P. John O'Rourke, Rosscarbery, died. R.I.P. |
| 16 | Women's Group outing to Cork Greyhound Stadium |
| 17 | Sean O'Donovan, Abbey Bar, took part in the Cork Autograss Racing Club event in |

*E1*
*Gretta's Prince won the All-Ireland 13.2 hand Pony Competition in Millstreet*

*E2*
*Local musicians, Sean & Sam Duignan, Elish Daly, Catriona, Rosarie, Denise and Danny Collins won awards at the Fleadh Ceoil ns hEireann*

Castletown-Kenneigh
22   New All-girl group Switch played at a fund-raiser for the Friends of Children of Chernobyl in the Pike Bar
24   Relics of St Therese in Kinsale – the nearest they came to Ross

### JULY

The Cross on Carrigfadda Hill was unveiled fifty years ago, in July 1961.
Priests present were; Fr. Willie Burke, Carrigfadda, Fr. Denis Barry and Fr. Cahalane, Drinagh.

4    Senior Citizen's outing to Kinsale
12   Elaine Flavin, Matthew Tuohy, Kevin Tuohy and Siobhan Walsh, all pupils of Mount St Michael's, left for Belarus to help in orphanages for sick children in Novinki
13   European Computer Driving Licence Graduation in Darrara
31   Ross Minors footballers lost their replay v. Doheny's by 2 goals

### AUGUST

8       Mass at Monument in Barley Hill to commemorate victims of quarry disasters
10-17   Ross Family Festival was a huge success despite broken weather
11      Official Opening by Michael Healy-Rae
14      Mass At Teampallain Fachtna
17      Ross Rag

*E3*
*Spancil Hill Lass owned by Thomas Herlihy*

*E4*
*Mark Tobin, Newmill*

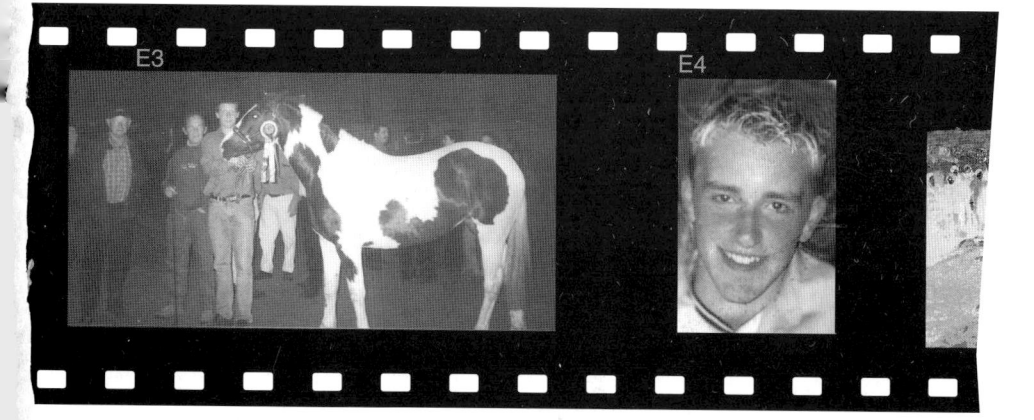

| | |
|---|---|
| 16-26 | Pitch & Putt AID Cancer Treatment for Pay Hayes Trophy |
| 17 | Gretta's Prince won the All-Ireland 13.2 hands Pony Competition in Millstreet. Other prize winners were Woodfield Pride and Spancil Hill Lass. |
| 19 | Ilen Rovers defeated Carbery Rangers for the third year in succession, 2-15 to 3-6 |
| 22 | Kate Keohane, Tullineaskey, died. R.I.P. |
| 25 | Ross Fair |
| 26 | Local musicians, Sean & Sam Duignan, Elish Daly, Catriona, Rosarie, Denise and Danny Collins won awards at the Fleadh Ceoil ns hEireann, All Ireland Final, held in Listowel. |

## SEPTEMBER

| | |
|---|---|
| | Mark Tobin, Newmill, left school to concentrate on a career playing golf. |
| 2 | Galway beat Cork in All-Ireland Football semi-final |
| 9 | Cork Minor Hurlers beat Galway in the All-Ireland Final |
| 11 | Day of Disaster – The World Trade Centre Twin Towers in New York were wrecked by hijacked planes. Thousands of lives were lost. |
| 14 | Official Day of Mourning for victims of Day of Disaster. |
| 15 | Historical Society outing to Fermoy |

*F1*
*Pitch & Putt President's Prize, l to r., Mary Mannion, Ann Walsh, Jerry Nagle, Micheal Paul Hicks and Jackie Kingston.*

*F2*
*Cononagh Races.*

| | |
|---|---|
| 16 | Pat Mannion's Captain's Prize Pitch & Putt Competition. Winner was Jim Canty |
| 17 | Family Festival Committee reported best-ever festival with profits of £5000 Rathbarry won a Gold Medal in Tidy Towns Competition |
| 19 | Parents AGM in Mount St Michael |
| 23 | Cononagh Races, revived after 17 years, were a great success |
| 24 | Fachtna O'Donovan, Lissard, died. R.I.P. Public Meeting to set up a Tidy Towns Group and Rosscarbery website was held in the Ross Lodge & Tavern |
| 25 | Rain fell after 23 days of Indian summer |
| 27 | Tom Galvin, Rathbarry, died. R.I.P. |
| 28, 29, 30 | First Rosscarbery History School |
| 30 | Michael Paul Hicks won the Pitch & Putt President's Prize |

*F3*
*Captain's Prize Pitch & Putt Competition, l. to r., Marian Hicks, Jim Canty, Pat Mannion, Robert Creedon.*

*F4*
*Johnny Dillon, Bachelor of Cononagh with MC Kevin Santry.*